The Battle
to Save the *Houston*

The Battle to Save the *Houston*

OCTOBER 1944 TO MARCH 1945

John Grider Miller

Naval Institute Press
Annapolis, Maryland

Library of Congress Cataloging in Publication Data

Miller, John Grider, 1935–
   The battle to save the *Houston*, October 1944 to March 1945.

   Bibliography: p.
   1. Houston (Cruiser : CL-81)   2. World War, 1939–1945—Naval operations, American.   3. World War, 1939–1945—Campaigns—Pacific Ocean.   I. Title.
D774.H65M55   1984   940.54'5973   85-314
ISBN 0-87021-276-1

Printed in the United States of America on acid-free paper ∞

Frontispiece: The USS *Houston* (CL-81), October 1944, by Richard Cross.

10   9   8   7   6   5   4

The whole fleet admires your persistence and guts.
—Halsey

Contents

viii   CONTENTS

Preface

Most war stories emphasize the skill and daring of a relatively few combatants whose actions, when combined with the vagaries of chance during dramatic scenes of battle, are key turning points in the fortunes of one side or the other. Like those stories, this one reenacts the heroic role of the second cruiser *Houston* and her crew, but it is more than just a battle of ship against aircraft, man against man. For a matter of days after she was first torpedoed, the *Houston* remained vulnerable to attack by implacable and determined Japanese adversaries; during this time she also found herself pitted against a new enemy as well, one as unmerciful as and more relentless than any human foe. Her battle against the sea, which threatened every hour of her return home, continued for months.

This is an account of an elemental struggle for survival, by individuals and by the crew of a fighting ship. It is a story of dangers shared and victories won, some at a terrible cost. And above all, it is a tribute to the indomitable human spirit, a tale as old as the art of seafaring itself.

Acknowledgments

It would have been impossible to recapture the *Houston*'s ordeal without the active assistance of many fine people. My involvement in the project began with the suggestion of Fred H. Rainbow, managing editor of the U.S. Naval Institute *Proceedings*. Dr. Dean C. Allard and his assistants in the Naval Historical Center's operational archives branch, Martha Crawley and Richard M. Walker, together with Paul Stillwell and Tomi Johnston of the U.S. Naval Institute's oral history collection, helped with my initial research. After examining their battle reports, damage reports, and oral history transcripts, I was prepared for the first of many conferences with Rear Admiral George H. Miller, USN (Ret.). Admiral Miller was the backbone of the project, bringing to it the same determination that characterized his battle to save the *Houston* forty years ago. His appeals brought in comments from more than seventy eyewitnesses. Most of these contributions came from members of the USS *Houston* Association, whose enthusiasm for the book has been reflected in the generous support offered by its four most recent presidents: Leslie M. Quay, James E. Potter, Lester J. Schnable, and John J. Skarzenski. I am particularly indebted as well to three other members of the *Houston* Association:

Anthony J. Caserta, the 1984 reunion chairman; Master Chief Journalist William J. Miller, USN (Ret.), for his photographic research, his assistance reading galleys, and his description of the actions of the fleet tug *Pawnee*; and William A. Kirkland, for his insights into the role played by the city of Houston and for his reconstruction of key battle scenes.

I was fortunate to have had superb editorial assistance, especially from Rear Admiral Miller, who kept pace with the progress of the manuscript and provided valuable technical comment on nearly every page; from Brigadier General Edwin H. Simmons, USMC (Ret.), for his insights both as author and as historian; and from my father, John S. Miller, who subjected the manuscript to the professional scrutiny that only a World War II veteran of the Destroyer New Construction desk, Bureau of Ships Code 514, could bring to bear. At the Naval Institute Press, Acquisitions Editor Richard R. Hobbs guided the book through the initial review and approval process, later making several key suggestions for streamlining the text, and Manuscript Editor Connie Buchanan saw to its refinement with technical skill and consistency that was matched only by the constancy of her encouragement and support.

A final acknowledgment goes to my wife Susan, who helped Admiral Miller keep the project moving during my long year overseas and who endured still another lonely year when, upon my return, I became a writer-in-exile.

All this assistance and support has been essential, but final responsibility for the views expressed here resides solely with me.

Foreword

This account of the struggle to salvage the damaged light cruiser *Houston* (CL 81) and bring her home from the western Pacific is the story of a band of determined men who would not give up their ship.

Conventional wisdom has it that a stricken warship lying dead in distant waters with her major weapons unusable and her hull severely battered is nothing but a clear liability. Why bother with damage control and put the lives of a crew on the line when it is easier to scuttle a badly damaged ship?

In wartime, decisions about the fate of disabled ships must take many factors into consideration. Which side has the upper hand when a ship becomes endangered? Can the crippled ship be kept afloat? Can her fires be brought under control? Can time and resources be risked to bring her safely into port? Not the least of these factors is the condition of the crew, their competence, and their will to survive.

From the outset of her travail, the *Houston*'s survival hung in a precarious balance. But this did not deter those responsible for the ship, for they had just begun to fight.

GEORGE H. MILLER
REAR ADMIRAL, U.S. NAVY (RET.)

The Battle
to Save the *Houston*

Prologue

Memorial Day, 1942, was a hard one for the people of Houston, Texas. Undercutting their annual rite of homage to the fallen of past wars was the stabbing personal pain of new loss in a new war. At that time, little encouraging news had arrived from abroad. The Allied nations were still on the defensive around the globe. America's first counteroffensive at Guadalcanal was more than two months away, and news of the operation would be long in coming. Early naval successes in the Coral Sea and off Midway Island would be subject to the same delays in wartime reporting. There was not much yet to cheer about. America could still lose this war.

The casualty lists were growing, and more and more Houston families were being touched by tragedy's cold fingers. In early March the heavy cruiser bearing their city's name had been listed by the U.S. Navy as missing and presumed lost. Details of her fate would not be known until the war's end, but it could be assumed that any survivors were in the hands of the Japanese. Now the entire community shared in the loss of war.

At dusk on that Memorial Day, more than one hundred thousand people assembled downtown on Main Street. In the center of the gathering, a handful of men in navy uniforms moved about, forming younger men into awkward ranks. One thousand volun-

teers from the Houston area were enlisting in the navy to replace the crew of the lost USS Houston. *It was a symbolic gesture, and more.*

There would be a message from the president. The townspeople waited, solemnly, for a shattered dream to be restored.

The light cruiser USS *Houston* (CL 81) was the third ship to carry the Texas city's name. The first was a 9,000-ton cargo ship, originally the SS *Liebenfels*, owned by the Hansa Line of Bremen, Germany. Scuttled by her German crew in the harbor of Charleston, South Carolina, when the United States entered World War I, the *Liebenfels* was subsequently salvaged by the U.S. Navy on 22 May 1917. She was redesignated the USS *Houston* (AK 1) and placed in commission on 3 July 1917, with Lieutenant Commander W. H. Lee of the Naval Reserve Fleet in command. She carried a complement of 10 officers and 134 enlisted men.

By the end of the war, seventeen months later, the *Houston* had made six Atlantic crossings with a variety of cargoes. She had also spent four months hauling coal from Wales to France. Assigned to the Naval Transportation service after the war, she capped four trips between East and West Coast ports with a single transpacific run to the Philippines before she returned to San Francisco's Mare Island Navy Yard for decommissioning on 23 March 1922. Six months later she was sold to Frank M. Warren of Portland, Oregon, for thirty-five thousand dollars.

In 1927, after a great deal of lobbying, the citizens of Houston managed to put their city's name on a new warship authorized under the terms of the Washington Naval Treaty. This "treaty cruiser" was constructed as hull no. 323 at Virginia's Newport News Shipbuilding and Dry Dock Company. Sponsored by Miss Elizabeth Holcombe, daughter of the mayor of Houston, the ship was launched on 7 September 1929.

The new *Houston* (CA 30) was a heavy cruiser, carrying nine 8-inch guns, four 5-inch guns, and six torpedo tubes. She was rated at 10,000 tons, but her actual displacement under a full combat load probably reached 14,000 tons. Her long sleek lines, clipper bow, and design speed of more than 32 knots made her a prized flagship. In less than twelve years she would fly the flags of seventeen admirals. During four voyages Franklin D. Roosevelt's presidential flag would fly from her main truck as well.[1]

After her commissioning on 17 June 1930, the *Houston*, with Captain Jesse B. Gay in command, made a shakedown cruise to Europe and her first visit to the city of Houston before she assumed duty as the flagship of the Asiatic station. Following more than two years in China and the Philippines, she returned to San Francisco. For most of the next six years, her cruises along the western seaboard were punctuated by periodic fleet exercises in Caribbean and Hawaiian operating areas.

The *Houston* returned to the Philippines in November 1940 to become the flagship of Admiral Thomas G. Hart, commander in chief of the Asiatic Fleet. The collection of aged ships then on the Asiatic station hardly qualified as an operational fleet. Even the *Houston* sorely needed modernization. Years of seagoing experience shared by the eight thousand men of the fleet tended to offset the materiel deficiencies. In time, however, the loss of many veteran sailors would be deeply felt, especially in the early dark days of the approaching war.[2]

In December 1941 Admiral Hart consolidated all his forces in the Philippines to face an imminent invasion. Within the month, however, Japanese pressure had increased to the point where further naval resistance was useless. Hart, acting under the governing Rainbow 5 war plan, withdrew southward with an Allied force whose new task became the near hopeless one of defending the vulnerable Malay Barrier.

By mid-February 1942 the Allies were isolated on Java. Two Japanese armadas closed in on them, setting the stage for the seven-hour Battle of the Java Sea. During the afternoon and evening of 27 February half the Allied force was destroyed, and its Dutch commander went down with his flagship. The Japanese sustained relatively light casualties.

The remaining Allied ships were ordered to break clear of the heavily patrolled Java Sea and move southward into the relative safety of the Indian Ocean. The *Houston*, in company with the Australian cruiser *Perth*, tried to round the western tip of Java and slip through the seemingly unguarded Sunda Strait. Late on the evening of 28 February, however, they encountered Rear Admiral Keno Kurita's Western Attack Force conducting a major amphibious landing at St. Nicolas Point, the gateway to Sunda Strait. Fifty-six Japanese troop transports were screened by an aircraft carrier, two heavy cruisers, one light cruiser, and a destroyer flotilla of about twelve ships.

The *Houston* and the *Perth*, with hope of escape now gone, decided to sell themselves dearly, attacking the line of transports while fighting off the screening force. The dark waters of the Java Sea glowed with the boiling phosphorescent wakes of eighty-seven torpedoes the Japanese had fired. Shortly after midnight the Australian cruiser went under, victimized by 8-inch-gun fire as well as torpedo hits.

The *Houston*, after one of the fiercest fights in naval history, would last but another half hour. She was dead in the water and sinking as her commanding officer, Captain Albert H. Rooks, ordered her abandonment—moments before he was killed by shrapnel. Only a third of her crew survived to find temporary refuge in the tepid waters of the Java Sea.

As she listed further to starboard, destroyer searchlights transfixed the slowly sinking cruiser in a pale, icy glare from stem to stern. Shells thudded into her repeatedly, and she continued to heel over until her yardarms dipped into the sea. Then a torpedo hit her amidships on the port side.

A survivor recalled the scene:

> After being subjected to so much punishment, the ship should have capsized instantly. Instead, the *Houston* tediously rolled back on an even keel. With decks awash, the proud ship paused majestically, while a sudden breeze picked up the Stars and Stripes, still firmly two-blocked on her mainmast, and waved them in one last defiant gesture. Then, with a tired shudder, the magnificent *Houston* vanished beneath the Java Sea.[3]

The full circumstances of the *Houston*'s heroic fight were not to be known, either to the U.S. Navy or to the American people, for several years. But even the reasonable supposition of heroism was enough to galvanize a remarkable public reaction in the United States.

The people of Houston bitterly mourned the loss of the ship they had come to regard as their own. So on that Memorial Day of 1942 the volunteers and their huge audience gathered on Main Street to hear Mayor Neal Pickett read a message from President Roosevelt:

> On this Memorial Day, all America joins with you who are gathered in proud tribute to a great ship and a gallant company of American officers and men. That fighting ship and those fighting Americans shall live forever in our hearts.
>
> I knew that ship and loved her. Her officers and men were my friends.
>
> When ship and men went down, still fighting, they did not go down to defeat. They had helped remove at least two cruisers and probably other vessels from the active list of the enemy's ranks. . . .
>
> The officers and men of the USS *Houston* drove a hard bargain. They sold their liberty and their lives most dearly.
>
> The spirit of these officers and men is still alive. That is being proved today in all Houston, in all Texas, in all America.
>
> Not one of us doubts that the thousand recruits sworn in today will carry on with the same determined spirit shown by the gallant men who have gone before them. . . .
>
> Our enemies have given us the chance to prove that there will be another USS *Houston*, and yet another USS *Houston* if that becomes necessary, and still another USS *Houston* as long as American ideals are in jeopardy. . . .
>
> The officers and men of the USS *Houston* have placed us all in their debt by winning a part of the victory which is our common goal. Reverently, and with all humility, we acknowledge this debt.
>
> To those officers and men, wherever they may be, we give our solemn pledge that the debt will be repaid in full.[4]

The swearing-in ceremony was conducted by Rear Admiral W. A. Glassford, recently returned from the Pacific. After the ceremony the men were marched to five special trains, which moved them quickly into the demanding new worlds of boot camp and advance speciality training. Only one of these thousand men would actually be assigned to the new USS *Houston* when she first went to sea.[5] Almost all the men were trained long before the ship was ready to receive them.

Nevertheless, the Houstonians still had a way of keeping tabs on their ship. A Houston banker named William A. Kirkland had been a junior naval officer in World War I. He had not been to sea since that time, but it was not difficult to activate his naval reserve commission in the grade of lieutenant commander. This enabled him to go to sea, although he trailed his contemporaries by at least twenty years of professional experience. He would begin his task with diligence as a special assistant to the executive officer of a new *Houston*.

Meanwhile, a number of townspeople had already called for their war bond purchases to be applied to the funding of another USS *Houston*. Some had approached fellow Houstonian Jesse H. Jones, the secretary of commerce, for assistance in replacing the lost ship.

It soon became evident that sympathy for the idea extended all the way to the White House. Two days after the swearing-in ceremony, Secretary of the Navy Frank Knox announced that one of four cruisers already under construction would be renamed the USS *Houston*.

By early October details of the redesignation had been completed, and Knox could announce that the light cruiser *Vicksburg*, then being built as hull no. 400 at the Newport News Shipbuilding and Dry Dock Company, would be renamed the *Houston* (CL 81).[6] This was in line with the navy's policy of perpetuating the names of ships lost in battle. It was also a clear reflection of Roosevelt's determination to avenge America's early losses, which he had made known so forcefully in his Memorial Day message.

The renaming, however, ran afoul of a lingering seagoing superstition. The precommissioning crew of the new *Houston*,

assembled in Newport News, were uneasy when they saw re-
minders—old name plates and stencils, for example—that the
ship's name had first been the *Vicksburg*. Changing the name
after her keel was laid was regarded as an invitation to bad
luck.[7]

Though the crew had no way of knowing it, a second announcement on the day of the *Vicksburg*'s renaming was
equally ominous: The heavy cruiser *Pittsburgh*, then building
at Quincy, Massachusetts, would be renamed the USS *Canberra*. Her fate would be closely linked with that of the *Houston*.

Back in Houston an elaborate fund-raising organization
was taking shape. The New Cruiser *Houston* Fund Drive was
headed by Charles I. Francis; the Harris County Victory Fund
Committee was chaired by Beverly D. Harris and George V. Ro-
tan; and the Harris County War Savings Committee was led by
Claud B. Hamill, whose wife was named as sponsor of the new
cruiser.[8] The fund drive involved a cross section of the citizenry,
including school children. More than two hundred thousand
individuals, firms, and organizations took part and inscribed
their names in an honor roll registration book to be carried on
board the new ship.[9]

The drive started on 30 November 1942, its goal to raise
over thirty-six million dollars in three weeks. On 21 December
the secretary of commerce delivered a check for over eighty-
five million dollars to the secretary of the navy with a suggestion that the surplus be used to fund a ship named the USS *San
Jacinto*, in commemoration of the battle that won Texas her independence.[10] Secretary of the Navy Knox agreed and made
the recommendation to President Roosevelt, who approved it
without hesitation.

CHAPTER ONE

In Harm's Way

The new USS *Houston* (CL 81), a light cruiser of the *Cleveland* class, was launched under a cloudless sky at Newport News on 19 June 1943. The ship's sponsor, Mrs. Claud Hamill, had good reason to swing the traditional bottle of champagne resolutely. A cousin of hers had been on board when the older *Houston* was lost in the Java Sea. She smashed the bottle hard against the cruiser's bow. Governor Coke Stevenson headed the visiting Texas delegation that shared the platform with Mrs. Hamill. People were leaning over the rail for a better view of the ship as she moved down the ways into the James River.

"There she goes. God bless her!" someone said hoarsely. The navy band struck up the first notes of "Anchors Aweigh."

Other notables from Houston, including Senator Tom Connally, crowded the platform. Minutes earlier, Secretary of Commerce Jesse Jones had reminded all present that the first cruiser *Houston* had made a goodwill visit to Japan more than ten years before. Jones went on to predict that the new *Houston* would also go to Japan, this time on a trip in behalf of the world, and that the Japanese would long remember her second visit.[1]

A little-noted sidelight of the launching ceremony was the

high-level attention given to a black Houstonian, Private Julius A. Allen of the U.S. Army. Private Allen, then doing stevedore work with the 381st Port Battalion in Newport News, had been a chauffeur in Houston before he joined the army. His former employer, Mrs. I. B. McFarland, had written to Secretary Knox with a personal request that Allen be admitted to the launching ceremony despite his low-ranking military status. She cited Allen's intense patriotism and his pride in the city, mentioning that he had bought a bond with his meager savings to help build the new *Houston*.[2]

The response was instantaneous. Two short-fused communications left the secretary's office. One went via the Bureau of Personnel, extending a direct invitation to Allen. The other went via the Bureau of Ships to the Newport News Shipbuilding and Dry Dock Company to ensure that Allen would not be denied admittance to the tightly guarded ceremony. Newspaper accounts of the launching may have missed a human-interest story by failing to note the lone khaki uniform with unadorned sleeves in the sea of navy brass.

Construction of the *Houston* continued through the fall of 1943. She was commissioned by Rear Admiral Felix Gygax, commandant of the Norfolk Navy Yard, on 10 December 1943. As the band played the national anthem, the national ensign, union jack, and commissioning pennant were hoisted together. After the pennant was lowered and the chaplain gave his invocation, Admiral Gygax turned the ship over to her first commanding officer, Captain William W. Behrens.

Captain Behrens read his orders and accepted the ship, then directed the executive officer to set the first watch. As the duty boatswain piped and called out, "Set the watch, first section," the navigator assumed the duty of officer of the deck. Notified that the watch had been set, the commanding officer ordered the ceremony to end with the playing of "Retreat."

The *Houston* was now a ship of the line. With a displacement of 10,000 tons and a design speed of 33 knots, she resembled her predecessor in some respects. But she was markedly different in others. Instead of nine 8-inch guns in three turrets, she carried twelve 6-inchers in four turrets. The CL 81 also lacked some of the comfortable living spaces that had been designed into the earlier *Houston*, called the "Little Flagship of the Fleet" while she sailed a total of 24,445 miles with the president on board. The new *Houston*, in contrast, would sail in harm's way, and very soon. Her main concern was to train her new crew to a fine edge in the use of the most modern weapons and equipment available.

As the crew prepared for a shakedown cruise in the Caribbean, some members received refresher training in their specialties. For his training, the ship's damage control officer, Lieutenant Commander George H. Miller, traveled to the Philadelphia Navy Yard. Heading the damage control school there was Commander Richard S. Mandelkorn, who had graduated from Annapolis first in his class in 1932, a year ahead of Miller.

Mandelkorn's philosophy with respect to the salvaging of crippled ships in combat areas was becoming the focus of intense debate within the navy. Early in the war the conventional procedure was to rescue the crew, then lay off and sink the battle-damaged ship. This was preferable to putting a healthy ship or several healthy ships at risk while towing and escorting a cripple back to safety for costly yard work. Despite the widespread appeal of this policy, Mandelkorn and other naval constructors were sickened by the number of American ships being sent to the bottom by American guns and torpedoes. They were convinced that even badly damaged ships could be returned to full duty far more quickly and cheaply than new-construction ships could be built.

"Just bring the hull back." These were Mandelkorn's last words to Miller. Miller never forgot.

On 1 February 1944 the *Houston* left Hampton Roads for Trinidad and a three-week shakedown cruise in the British West Indies. The full array of ship's systems would be thoroughly checked out—as would the crew, three-fifths of whom were going to sea for the first time. The crew drilled day and night to train for every situation they might conceivably face in combat. Captain Behrens and Commander Miller set a demanding and relentless pace to the dismay of the inexperienced. The older hands, however, recognized the full schedule of drills as but a tentative sample of things to come once the ship moved into a theater of war.

The *Houston* suffered slight storm damage during the shakedown cruise. In the process of repairing this, both at sea and during a six-week post-shakedown availability period, Commander Miller made a detailed assessment of his overall damage control capability. He decided that it was clearly inadequate. Captain Behrens agreed.

The existing allowance of equipment gave him only half of the emergency breathing devices he felt were really needed. Without them damage control parties could not function in smoke-filled compartments. There had been a vivid demonstration of this during a fire-fighting drill when a sailor had been overcome by smoke. An officer with more courage than sense immediately went to the rescue—without a breathing device—and quickly became a victim himself. His condition only compounded the problem for the trained and equipped rescue party that went into action moments later and saved both men.

Miller lacked an adequate supply of lumber for shoring up damaged sections of the hull, bulkheads, decks, and overheads. He was also unhappy with his standard-issue welding equipment, which was incapable of the heavy-duty work he visualized as part of an extreme damage control situation. The list of shortcomings was long.

The *Houston* was scheduled to spend two weeks in Boston to test her main engines and to calibrate her compasses and direction finders before she sailed for the Pacific. In Boston, Miller calculated, the situation could be rectified. He gathered his damage control assistants and told them exactly what additional equipment was required to do the job right. Within two weeks, by one means or another, he would have everything he wanted.

On 16 April 1944 the *Houston*, now a part of Cruiser Division 14, left Boston for San Diego via the Mona Passage and the

Panama Canal, sailing in company with the cruisers *Vincennes* and *Miami*. On 1 May she departed from San Diego for Pearl Harbor, which she reached in six days. During the next two weeks she made her final preparations for combat, spending a great deal of time on the Hawaiian naval gunfire ranges and on never-ending drills in damage control. Miller became even more of a demanding taskmaster as combat duty neared, winning more respect than affection as he strove to convince his men that the survival of the ship could well hinge on their special competence.

On 23 May the *Houston* was under way for Majuro Atoll in the Marshall Islands. She was part of a task force that included her cruiser division, two battleships, seven destroyers, and a fast minelayer. Reaching Majuro eight days later, the *Houston*'s crew got their first look at the low sand mounds and clustered palm trees that characterize the Pacific atolls. This was a particularly desolate sight for sailors fresh from the Atlantic and the Caribbean who were accustomed to putting into real ports when they returned to shore.

At the time, however, the prospect of liberty ports was secondary at best. There was a war on, and the *Houston* was finally in it, as part of Vice Admiral Marc A. Mitscher's celebrated Task Force 58.

This task force was the striking force of Vice Admiral Raymond A. Spruance's Fifth Fleet, which was then preparing for operations to support the recapturing of the Marianas. While the Fifth Fleet operated in the western Pacific, Admiral William F. Halsey and his Third Fleet staff were back in Hawaii, planning for still later landings in the Philippines. These landings had been slated to begin on southern Mindanao by mid-November 1944 and to be followed by a landing at Leyte Gulf on 20 December.

When the numbered fleet commanders and their staffs traded places, the task designators would change. Task Force 58 would become Task Force 38. But the ships would remain the same.

No matter who called the signals at any given time, Task

Force 58/38 constituted the most formidable armada ever assembled. Whenever its subordinate task groups rendezvoused
in a single formation at sea, the full task force easily covered an
area of ten by forty miles and had a reach that extended hundreds of miles—to the range limits of its carrier-based aircraft.
With its task groups operating independently, the force could
cover vast stretches of the western and southern Pacific, supporting offensive operations on land and seeking decisive engagement with the Imperial Japanese Navy.

In just over two years since the Allied defeat in the Java
Sea, the fortunes of war had shifted markedly, if not yet de-
cisively, against the Japanese. Their westward expansion had
been checked, and American forces were flooding back toward
the Japanese home islands with twin drives headed by Admiral
Chester Nimitz and General Douglas MacArthur across the
central and southern Pacific.

The Japanese fleet had been badly mauled in the battles of
Midway Island and the Coral Sea, but it still posed a threat
when its forces were consolidated closer to home. For operations in the western Pacific, the Japanese Navy had organized a
combined fleet under Admiral Soemu Toyoda. Its two principal
operating forces were the Third Fleet, under Vice Admiral Jisa-
buro Ozawa, and the Second Fleet, under Vice Admiral Takeo
Kurita.

Japan's severely depleted naval aviation capability rested
with her Third Fleet in the form of three carrier divisions that
had screening cruisers and destroyers. Kurita's Second Fleet,
on the other hand, was essentially a surface force, consisting of
five battleships (two with 18-inch guns, the largest ever), ten
heavy cruisers, one light cruiser, and twelve destroyers.

The Japanese also had a training fleet and three small "area"
fleets made up of cruisers and destroyers. These four fleets remained separated from the main fighting power of the Combined Fleet, however, and could not be counted on for action in
the western Pacific.

On 6 June 1944, while the world's attention was focused on

the beaches of Normandy half a world away, the *Houston* quietly sortied from Majuro with Task Group 58.4, as part of the cruiser/destroyer screen for the aircraft carriers *Essex*, *Langley*, and *Cowpens*. Within two days, bogeys—contacts presumed hostile—began to appear on the *Houston*'s radar screens. Nearly two weeks would pass, however, before Japanese aircraft would first be sighted.

By 0400 on 12 June the task group had reached its launch point for heavy air strikes against Saipan and Pagan in the Marianas. The strikes began at dawn, and by 1100 the *Houston* had received her first special assignment. The task group commander ordered the cruiser to send both her OS2U Kingfisher scout seaplanes, escorted by two carrier-based fighters, to rescue downed carrier pilots in the vicinity of Pagan Island.

The American aviators, who had managed to inflate their life rafts, were quickly spotted. Both Kingfishers landed in the water nearby. Then problems began. The sea began to make up, and one aircraft soon capsized as the waves grew higher. The other Kingfisher could do little but stand by and serve as a marker for the surface search-and-rescue party, consisting of two destroyers that had left the task group formation and were proceeding toward Pagan. While they waited to be rescued, the downed fliers were mindful of the fact that the remaining Kingfisher also served as a convenient and attractive marker for any Japanese ships or aircraft that might enter the area. By daybreak on 13 June the destroyers had made their rendezvous and returned to the task group formation, reporting that all fliers—both rescuers and rescued—were safe on board. Unfortunately the second Kingfisher had sunk in the interim, but this was regarded as a better-than-equal tradeoff, for the aircraft could soon be replaced.

Heavy air strikes continued. More bogeys lit up the radar screens on the afternoon of 13 June, and at least one hostile aircraft was downed by planes of the task group's combat air patrol. After they had recovered their strike aircraft at day's end, the ships of Task Group 58.4 left the area, heading for next morning's fueling rendezvous with the fleet oilers *Sabine, Kaskaskia*, and *Cimarron*.

When they had topped off their fuel tanks, the ships of the task group made a rendezvous with Task Group 58.1, en route to launch positions for the next day's strike against Iwo Jima and Chichi Jima in the Bonin Islands. In these new positions the vessels were closer to Tokyo than any American surface ships had been up to that point in the war except for the aircraft carrier *Hornet* group, which had taken Colonel Jimmy Doolittle's bombers to launch the surprise raid on Tokyo early in the war. The Doolittle Raid had been a hit-and-run venture, more valued for its impact upon the Japanese, who were not accustomed to having their homeland attacked, than for the physical damage it exacted, which did not amount to much. This time, however, the carrier task forces were moving into formerly Japanese-controlled waters to stay. In the early critical hours of the amphibious operation against Saipan, Japanese air strength in the Bonins had to be pinned down to protect the landing and buildup ashore of American forces.

By noon on 15 June the *Houston*'s task group was up against another enemy—the weather. The sea made up as the wind increased to 30 knots and the ceiling lowered from 4,000 feet to near zero. Rain squalls swept across the area. Despite these conditions the carriers maneuvered to launch a successful afternoon strike. They recovered all their aircraft by dusk.

Bad weather continued through the night as the task groups sought favorable launch positions for the next day's strikes. The weather did not break until the afternoon of the sixteenth, but improved conditions came early enough to permit one final raid on Iwo Jima and, once again, recovery of all strike aircraft before sunset.

The two task groups then set a southerly course, heading for a rendezvous with the rest of Task Force 58 that was scheduled for 18 June. On the way, to sow some confusion about their destination, they launched a diversionary strike against the air installations on the western side of Pagan.

By noon on 19 June the reassembled Task Force 58 was under heavy air attack for about six hours, but only one of the Japanese strikes was directed at Task Group 58.4. Fifteen of the sixteen Zeke aircraft were shot down in air-to-air dogfights by the task group's combat air patrol. The sixteenth, however, disappeared from the ships' radar screens and was unaccounted for.

Suddenly, the missing Zeke emerged from a cloud bank and dove on the carrier *Essex*, dropping a small bomb nearby. When the pilot recovered from his dive, he found himself skimming across the water.

Commander Charles O. Cook, the *Houston*'s navigator and officer of the deck during general quarters, had a ringside seat about two thousand yards off the starboard beam of the *Essex*:

> . . . I may be wrong but I have no recollection of any shots being fired at this target up to this point by any ship. . . . With this little guy inside the screen and below the mastheads of the larger ships, we would have been more likely to hit ourselves than him. He didn't waste any time getting out, zigging once left and once right in sharp jerks and bouncing once up and once down like a rubber ball, making it virtually impossible to take aim on him in any event. The screen ahead opened fire as he shot over their mastheads, but it is unlikely that their bullets ever caught up. In perhaps ten seconds from my first glimpse, I lost sight of him. . . . From his size, speed, and maneuverability, he appeared to be a fighter. The pilot was clearly well qualified.[3]

Since no one had been hurt by his attack, the audacity of the lone Japanese pilot soon became the subject of banter about the *Houston*'s decks. The crew's first close glimpse of the enemy had been a sobering one, however. Up to this point the notion had prevailed among them that most of Japan's best pilots had already been shot out of the sky. But now it was clear that there were still some very good fliers around. And to a man, the *Houston*'s crew realized that it only took one good torpedo launched by one good pilot to score a devastating hit on their ship.

Most of Task Force 58 did not realize it at the time, but the battle they had just fought, from 16 to 20 June, would mark one of the turning points of the war in the Pacific.

The effectiveness of American air strikes against the Bonins and elsewhere had prevented the Japanese from supporting the defenders of Saipan with planes from airfields that ringed the beleaguered island. To compensate, Ozawa had launched his largest carrier-based air strikes of the war against Task Force 58. All three carrier divisions of his Third Fleet had been committed in what became known as the Battle of the Philippine Sea—or, less officially, "The Marianas Turkey Shoot." The results had been one-sided, with over four hundred Japanese aircraft destroyed and relatively slight American losses.

In time, American intelligence officers would learn more about the nature of that Japanese defeat. Three enemy carriers had been sunk during the battle, two by American submarines and one by American carrier aircraft. Even more telling than the loss of three major ships, however, was the near-total destruction of the Japanese aircraft groups that had been embarked in the ships of the three carrier divisions. By the end of the battle on 20 June, only forty aircraft and one hundred pilots remained on board the surviving enemy carriers.

The Japanese soon recognized that the task of rebuilding the devastated carrier groups was overwhelming. Consequently, between June and October 1944 the Japanese fleet organization—with its backbone of naval aviation all but shattered—would undergo a major overhaul as Admiral Toyoda tried desperately to regroup his Combined Fleet. In the course of this reorganization, Kurita's surface forces would become virtually the last if not the best hope of stopping the Americans.

Meanwhile, the *Houston* moved eastward to rejoin the Marianas campaign. In addition to screening for carriers once more, she had her first try at shore bombardment. On the island of Rota she attacked several structures, including a radio station, some barracks, and a factory. At Guam she shared credit for sinking a tug and a small cargo ship and for destroying five gasoline tanks in a harbor. She also attacked an air strip with naval gunfire, destroying ten to twelve aircraft on the ground, the field's gun emplacements, and all but two of its fuel tanks.

In mid-July the *Houston* made a brief stop in Eniwetok for fuel and supplies. She returned to the Marianas to support operations against Guam and Tinian, and early in August screened for carriers in the fourth raid on the Bonin Islands. Then she returned to Eniwetok for two weeks of ship upkeep and resupply. The end of this period coincided with the return of Admiral Halsey and his Third Fleet staff to the western Pacific. It was their turn again to climb into the operational saddle, but, as expected, the horses did not change. The *Houston* was now a part of Task Force 38.

The crew expected a return to the seakeeping routine that was becoming familiar after three months: steaming in battle formation; engaging in gunnery exercises and occasional shore bombardment; refueling at sea; and seeking relatively secure anchorages for upkeep. The men were growing leaner, tougher, and more self-confident as they adjusted to the unrelenting operational pace.

This time, however, things were different. The changeover of fleet commanders appeared to be bringing a new direction and a fresh impetus to the war in the western Pacific. Something was definitely up, and it had to do with Halsey's return.

CHAPTER TWO

The Showdown Commences

By September of 1944, Bull Halsey was already a legend. He was Nimitz's favorite fighting admiral, and he had won the strongest loyalty of his fighting men at sea. He was probably the American admiral most hated by the Japanese as well— particularly for his flamboyant if somewhat inaccurate prophesies about the early collapse of his foes and his subsequent ride through Tokyo astride Emperor Hirohito's white horse. The citizens of Reno, Nevada, rallying to the boast, had presented Halsey with a handsome saddle to use for the occasion.

But Halsey was all business now. He had brought from the Hawaiian planning sessions a set of instructions that had been taken from Nimitz's operation plan. They tasked Halsey, first of all, to cover and support the forces of the southwest Pacific in the seizure and occupation of objectives in the central Philippines. And they assigned him two other missions. He was to destroy any Japanese naval and air forces operating within the Philippines objective area or threatening that area, and was to protect Allied air and sea lines of communication along the central Pacific axis.

In other words, Halsey's prime concern was the support and protection of the vulnerable amphibious forces that were then being assembled to recapture the Philippines. But Halsey tended to cherish his own priorities. He longed for a decisive engagement that would result in the final destruction of the Japanese fleet. Accordingly, a new line crept into the operation plan that represented both Halsey's strengths and his ambitions: "In case opportunity for destruction of [a] major portion of the enemy fleet [is offered] or can be created, such destruction becomes the primary task."[1]

Halsey had armed himself with a license to go for the throat.

At this stage of the war, Japan's naval strength was decidedly inferior to that of the United States. The combined strengths of the American Third and Seventh Fleets exceeded one thousand ships, roughly four hundred of them amphibious. By contrast, Admiral Toyoda's Combined Fleet, after the treatment it had received in the Battle of the Philippine Sea, numbered only seventy-six combatants. Toyoda's ships were now divided into two task forces. The first was the so-called Main Body, commanded by Vice Admiral Ozawa. It would continue to be based in Japan's Inland Sea. Ozawa's crippled carrier force was racing against time to repair its ships and to replace its lost pilots and aircraft before the next American attack. The Main Body included the No. 2 Diversion Attack Force, under Vice Admiral Kiyohide Shima.

The more potent of the two task forces was the curiously named No. 1 Diversion Attack Force, commanded by Vice Admiral Takeo Kurita. With enough power to be considered a main body force, it was geared for surface engagement at long range. Kurita's force had maintained its base of operations at Lingga Anchorage, near Singapore.

By this time the Japanese high command had, in effect, drawn its final defensive line southward from the main islands of Honshu and Kyushu through the Ryukyus, Formosa, and the Philippines. The badly outnumbered Japanese fleet had a valuable trump card to play from this consolidated position—land-based aviation, which could operate from scores of airfields along and behind the defensive line. Until the Americans could uncover landing fields of their own, the task of gaining air superiority throughout the region would fall almost entirely upon their carrier-based aircraft.

Against this background, with the prospect of landings at Leyte Gulf nearly four months away, Halsey sent Task Force 38 back into action in late August 1944.

Through the end of August and most of September, new strikes were directed throughout the Philippines. Some of the early attacks in this region brought surprisingly weak resistance, and Halsey soon concluded that the timetable for the assault on Leyte could be advanced two months from its scheduled 20 December D day. Halsey made the recommendation to MacArthur, who went on to secure the hasty approval of the Joint Chiefs of Staff. Slightly over a month now remained for replanning and for marshaling forces and supplies to conduct one of the major landings of the war.

Other decisions were required as well. A landing at Peleliu would proceed as scheduled on 15 September. The assault on Yap Island, in the Carolines, would be canceled.

Another complication arose when U.S. forces seized Ulithi Atoll without resistance on 21 September. This large anchorage could easily contain all the ships of Task Force 38 at one time. It had the added advantage of being a thousand miles closer to Leyte than Eniwetok, its predecessor as the main base of the Pacific Fleet west of Hawaii. Amid quickening preparations for the Leyte landings, the massive American logistics effort shifted westward.

The somber prospect of new American attacks did not diminish Japanese propaganda efforts, which took a new tack after an earlier attempt to downplay an unrelieved series of setbacks. The new approach was predicated on the strong sentiment that the American fleet could be lured far enough westward to overextend itself. At that point it would be vulnerable to counterattacks from Japanese air and naval surface forces.

The Japanese, no less than Halsey, saw a showdown developing close to their home waters. If they lost, their forces strung along the chain of islands leading to Japan would be subject to defeat in detail, falling one by one. If they won, on the other hand, they might recover from all their reverses in the Pacific.

The Japanese plan for the defense of the Philippines assigned a central role to Kurita's No. 1 Diversion Attack Force, which would strike the American surface force that would be protecting the anticipated landing. After it had annihilated this covering force, the Diversion Attack Force could attend to the destruction of amphibious ships at the landing site.

Despite its name, Ozawa's Main Body would actually serve as a decoy to draw Halsey's fast carrier forces northward, away from the landing operations. The Japanese aircraft carriers, with few planes left on their flight decks, would be hard pressed to protect themselves from air attack and would not have enough escort ships to provide an adequate surface screening force. In a word, the mission, meant to buy precious time for Kurita, was suicidal.

As Japanese planning reached its final stages, Halsey was already beginning to position Task Force 38 for his preliminary air strikes against the airfields in the Philippines.

Time had run out for Toyoda. The Japanese fleet could not be rebuilt. The Imperial Navy saw clearly the total sacrifice that Ozawa's force might have to make. But there was no longer a choice.

Publicly, Japanese naval officials remained confident. In mid-September Navy Minister Yonai told the parliamentarians that the Combined Fleet was "imbued with a burning fighting spirit to crush the enemy at the earliest opportunity." Privately, however, Toyoda's chief of staff was doubtful. Penning his comments on the defense plan, he wrote candidly that Toyoda's force "may be called our last line of home defense. . . . It must make a desperate effort to defeat the enemy."[2]

Assigned to Rear Admiral Bogan's Task Group 38.2, the *Houston* sailed 30 August from Eniwetok to screen for air attacks on the Palaus on 6 September. After these air strikes the cruiser joined with destroyers for naval gunfire attacks on Angaur, Ngesebus, and Peleliu in preparation for amphibious landings. After screening for subsequent strikes against airfields and shipping in the Philippines, the *Houston* returned to Peleliu and gave naval gunfire support to forces ashore from 17 to 19 September. By month's end she had replenished her magazines with ammunition from Saipan and proceeded to the newly captured anchorage at Ulithi.

It was typhoon season in the Pacific—a fact that would have a major bearing on the operations of the Third Fleet during the autumn of 1944. Two of Task Force 38's four carrier battle groups were operating away from Ulithi when the typhoon of 3–4 October struck. Vice Admiral McCain's Task Group 38.1 had sortied from Seeadler Harbor at Manus Island, well to the east. Rear Admiral Davison's Task Group 38.4, which had left Manus on 24 September, was still covering the Peleliu operation. The remaining two groups, anchored in the massive Ulithi lagoon, were vulnerable to the storm. Since the necklace of low-lying islands around the lagoon offered relatively little protection from wind and wave action, Halsey ordered those two groups out of the anchorage, where they might have a chance of ducking the typhoon.

After the storm passed, the ships returned to the Ulithi lagoon to find that a great deal of lighterage—a total of seventy-nine landing craft—had been lost. Although this complicated their efforts, the task groups managed to replenish and, on the afternoon of 6 October, they sortied from Ulithi on the tail of the typhoon.

As the storm, packing 100-knot winds near the center, moved along a track to the northwest, Halsey maneuvered his forces behind it, taking advantage of the cover and concealment it offered. He even gave the typhoon a navy task designator—Task Force 0—as weather forecasters and navigators worked hand-in-glove to trail the storm at a close but respectful distance.[3]

The *Houston* sortied with Rear Admiral Bogan's Task Group 38.2, which sailed in company with Halsey in the battleship

New Jersey. Mitscher, in the carrier *Lexington*, accompanied Rear Admiral Sherman's Task Group 38.3 toward a rendezvous of all four task groups, 375 miles west of the Marianas. Once pulled together, the formation was indeed formidable. It consisted of eight large aircraft carriers, eight more light carriers, six new battleships, six heavy cruisers, nine light cruisers, and fifty-eight destroyers.

Task Force 38's fueling group of nine fleet oilers also appeared at the rendezvous point and spent the entire day of 8 October topping off all the combatants, a difficult task. Even though the center of the typhoon was far to the north, the seas were still heavy and confused and there were large swells. The crews of the oilers worked with decks awash in a stern test of seamanship and sea legs.

The first objective of Task Force 38 was to neutralize Okinawa and smaller islands in the Ryukyus chain through air strikes. The objective was valid but it posed considerable risk. Halsey would be operating more than twelve hundred miles from the nearest American-held bases, Saipan and Ulithi. In preparing to penetrate the final line of Japanese defense, he appeared to be putting his head in the noose formed by a ring of air bases that ran from Iwo Jima through Korea and the home islands, back through China, and down to the Philippines. All these places were within aircraft range of Okinawa, which was a formidable base in itself. Okinawa had not yet been attacked in the war.

To minimize his chances of getting caught in the noose, Halsey created a diversion by attacking Marcus Island, north of Iwo Jima, en route to Okinawa. Using a special task group of three heavy cruisers and six destroyers, he conducted a day-long shore bombardment on 9 October after approaching undetected behind a weather front. He also used smoke screens and decoys to confuse Japanese radar operators and to leave the impression that a somewhat larger bombardment group was preparing in earnest for an imminent landing.

The air strikes on Okinawa began at dawn on 10 October and quickly overwhelmed the defenders. Planes from Task

Groups 38.2 and 38.3 hit the northernmost installations on Okinawa and the offshore island of Ie Shima. Task Groups 38.1 and 38.4 concentrated on the capital city of Naha, its harbor, and its surrounding airfields. Lucrative shipping targets presented themselves in harbors and anchorages off Okinawa's western coast. Barracks, docks, hangars, warehouses, storage dumps as well as airfields were demolished. Japanese broadcasts reported that the whole city of Naha was destroyed.

So far Halsey had prevented the Japanese from tightening the noose. Japanese opposition in the air had been inconsequential. About twenty defending aircraft had been shot down over the Ryukyus, and only three had managed to get anywhere near the Task Force 38 operating area, where they all were knocked out of the sky.

Later on 10 October, as the American task force began its retirement toward Luzon and another refueling rendezvous, more bogeys began to appear on the ships' radar screens. Few of these actually ventured into visual contact range, and only one came close enough to launch an attack. It was unsuccessful. The Japanese were beginning to react as they recovered from the shock of the devastating raid on Okinawa. Admiral Toyoda, feeling that the long-awaited showdown was about to begin in earnest, decided to direct operations from his temporary headquarters on Formosa, a likely target for future American air strikes. The Japanese government, on the other hand, seized upon Task Force 38's high-speed retirement toward Luzon as an opportunity to proclaim a great victory. Such grandiose claims may have confused the world at large for a time, but the defenders of Formosa and the Philippines had no illusions about American weakness in the western Pacific.

Halsey planned a strike on Luzon's Aparri airfield to mask his intention of conducting a major strike on Formosa, the strongest and best-developed Japanese base outside the home islands. The most significant aspect of the Aparri strike on 11 October, however, proved to be the day's grace it gave to the defenders of Formosa.

Toyoda and Vice Admiral Shigeru Fukudome, commander

of the Sixth Base Air Force, had about two hundred thirty operational aircraft on Formosa. These could be reinforced by an elite "T" (Typhoon) Force of twin-engine Betty torpedo planes from the home island of Kyushu. The land-based aircraft on Formosa had been shadowing Task Force 38 ever since the Okinawa strike, so Halsey's feint against Luzon had not fooled the Japanese.

Nevertheless, Task Force 38 was unopposed on 12 October as it made a high-speed run-in to aircraft launch positions ranging from fifty to ninety miles east of Formosa. To gain local air superiority, a fighter sweep was launched an hour before sunrise. First light brought excellent flying weather for the start of a three-day effort to put Formosa out of business.

The furious tempo of operations matched that of the Okinawa strike. The first day saw 1,378 sorties flown, from all four task groups. Japanese ground installations were heavily damaged and Fukudome's headquarters ceased to exist, although Fukudome himself survived the attack.

Because Japanese aviators had more than they could handle in the skies over Formosa, the American task groups at sea remained unmolested during the day. An occasional "snooper" approached the ships, taking care to remain well beyond the range of their antiaircraft guns.

By sunset on 12 October all returning strike aircraft had been recovered. The *Houston*'s task group steamed about eighty-five miles off the east coast of Formosa in battle formation Five Victor Five, with the flagship and five carriers inside a circle of screening ships. The other three groups of Task Force 38 steamed to the south. A 20-knot wind was blowing from the northeast, and the sea was rough. Even though the sky was eighty percent overcast, visibility remained fair.

At 1856, a few minutes after sunset, inbound Japanese aircraft were picked up by radar. The *Houston* sounded general quarters, and sailors dogged down the watertight doors and hatches to set material readiness condition AFIRM. The crew did not have long to wait at their battle stations. This time the bogeys—eventually identified as Bettys from the "T" Force—were coming all the way in. Within two minutes of the initial report, the Mark 4 radars of the forward and after 5-inch-gun directors had each picked up an incoming raid. The range was twenty miles and closing. Four minutes later the advance range of the forward director's target had closed to 16,000 yards. Two of the 5-inch mounts under that director's control commenced firing. Thirty seconds later, two of the after 5-inch mounts opened fire on another target that was crossing astern at a range of 14,000 yards.

The forward mounts scored first. A huge fireball blossomed, lighting up the sky like an orange star before it split into the blazing remnants of two distinct aircraft, which crashed separately into the sea.

The target astern was also downed, within minutes, but the Japanese aircraft pressed their attack close aboard for another half hour. To the men at battle stations topside, it seemed as though the pilots did not realize how closely they approached their darkened targets. Aircraft swarmed around the ships at altitudes of 50 feet and lower. As they moved within range of shipboard automatic weapons, the planes were chased across the night sky by streams of tracers from the 40mm- and 20mm-gun mounts of the *Houston* and other screening ships.

At 1925 two aircraft suddenly appeared close aboard on the port bow. One released a torpedo that dropped into the water with a distinct splash. The *Houston* twisted hard to port, using both rudder and engines, and avoided being hit. The torpedo streaked past and disappeared into the night.

One of the two aircraft continued astern and was soon gone from view as well. But the other swooped close over the stern, banked sharply to the left, and zoomed back in a suicidal run along the *Houston*'s starboard side. Firing at almost point-blank range, the gunners in the 40mm and 20mm mounts virtually hammered the plane to pieces. These automatic weapons had nonexplosive projectiles that did not normally produce the spectacular "flamers" that are the hallmark of the 5-inch round.

This time, however, fire broke out in the plane's cockpit, and another flaming orange star lit up the sky before falling into the sea just beyond the starboard bow of the *Houston*. As this was taking place, three or four aircraft were brought under fire by the *Houston*'s other 40mm and 20mm mounts. At least one of these planes was also shot down.

By 1930 the evening's first attack was over. Surviving Japanese aircraft retired singly, in all directions, taking up orbits around the task group at ranges that varied from fifteen to forty miles. From time to time a single plane would attempt to dart into the task group formation, but the Japanese did not try to rendezvous and form another organized attack. During this lull the shipboard radar operators found it relatively easy to track the occasional single-aircraft feints. The *Houston*'s 5-inch gunners managed to down one of the aircraft at a range of 5,000 yards.

A new phase of the evening's activity began when the Japanese tried to light up the *Houston*'s task group. Aircraft dropped eight parachute flares in a 180-degree arc to silhouette the ships with eerily effective back lighting. But the follow-up air attack never came. Several other illumination efforts concentrating on the carrier *Hancock* also failed to trigger the anticipated air attacks.

After a while it appeared that the Japanese had given up on coordinated large-scale attacks for the evening. Instead, their aircraft began to form in pairs outside the range of antiaircraft guns. One pilot would begin his run-in for an attack, and his wingman would drop metallic decoy material in an attempt to confuse the ships' fire-control radars. The technique was supposed to create multiple phony images on the radar screens, masking the images of the attacking aircraft themselves, but it didn't work. The radar operators of the task force were neither deceived nor prevented from acquiring and tracking the real aircraft.

This became apparent to the attacking pilots once they had closed to a range of ten miles or so. At that point they were taken under fire by the 5-inch mounts, which were operating under radar control. Realizing that they had been pinpointed, and that things were likely to get hotter if they continued flying toward an attack point, the pilots lost heart and turned back.

By midnight the ships of the task group began to lay smoke screens, so that the enemy's illuminating flares would not work. Within a half hour the ships' radar screens were finally clear of bogeys, and remained so for the rest of the night.

The attacking aircraft returned to Formosa with their formations punished and thinned. Fukudome later admitted to losing forty-two planes in these raids, which had left the *Houston*'s task group undamaged. The *Houston*'s gunners had a strong claim to eight downed aircraft—an impressive showing in their first real air defense action, especially since it took place at night. A review of Japanese aerial tactics by analysts in the *Houston*'s combat information center turned up something unsettling, however: The very aggressiveness of the ship's antiaircraft defense appeared to be highlighting the ship as a target.

Japanese pilots, lacking radar for target acquisition, were directing their night attacks toward the sources of the heaviest 40mm and 20mm tracer fire. Such heavy close-in fire by the *Houston* had evidently provided a beacon for the lone torpedo attack she had managed to evade. Since the automatic weapons did not have their own radar fire control systems, however, their gunners would still have to rely on tracers for adjusting their fire against attacking aircraft. They recognized the problem but did not have a ready solution at the time.

Even though the on-board euphoria over the *Houston*'s fine showing was not dampened by the post-attack analysis, it was quickly overtaken by the demands of the following day. On 13 October the task group began launching aircraft at 0614, a half hour before sunrise. All four task groups put nearly a thousand sorties in the air before noon. Several previously unknown airfields on Formosa were discovered and attacked. Japanese opposition was negligible all day. By sunset all aircraft from the

Houston's task group had been recovered without incident. Within a few minutes, however, bogeys were again reported closing on the formation under conditions that were essentially unchanged from the previous night: overcast skies, winds from the northeast at 30 knots, and no moon.

The *Houston*'s combat information center had picked up two bogeys at twenty miles, then handed off the contact to the after 5-inch-gun director, which began tracking in full radar control. As the target closed to 9,500 yards, the after 5-inch mounts opened fire. The plane continued closing to about six thousand yards before abruptly turning back, pursued by fire from the *Houston*. Suddenly, a twin-engine aircraft appeared on the port bow, close aboard. As it crossed from port to starboard, it took multiple hits from the 40mm and 20mm mounts and decided to retire.

After counting up the previous night's losses, the Japanese seemed to lack their earlier staying power. No further contacts materialized that evening, and the *Houston*'s task group congratulated themselves on another shutout.

The other groups were not so fortunate. Over in Task Group 38.4, the aircraft carrier *Franklin* had been attacked by four low-flying Bettys as she recovered aircraft at twilight. Three were knocked down and the fourth had been set aflame just before it crashed into the *Franklin*'s flight deck, skidding in a fiery ball across the deck and over the side. Despite this spectacular crash, damage to the *Franklin* was relatively minor.

In Vice Admiral McCain's Task Group 38.1, however, the heavy cruiser *Canberra*—which had been renamed on the same day in 1942 as the *Houston*—suffered a harsher fate. Shortly after sundown on 13 October, while the carriers of that task group were still recovering their aircraft, eight Japanese torpedo bombers came in low out of the twilight sky, undetected by radar. Six of them were downed by antiaircraft fire from the screen of cruisers and destroyers. One of the two surviving aircraft launched a torpedo that struck the *Canberra* below the armor belt around her hull. Flames flashed as high as her masthead, and twenty-three men died instantly. About forty-five hundred tons of floodwater poured in through the large hole in her side as damage control parties worked frantically to seal off the affected compartments and control the flooding.

The *Canberra* lay dead in the water, incapable of helping herself out of danger. She did not appear to be sinking, but she was more than a thousand miles from the nearest friendly base and less than a hundred miles from the nearest hostile one. More air attacks from Formosa were only forty minutes away when the report of the damaged ship reached Fukudome. The *Canberra*'s luck had run out on Friday the thirteenth.

At first glance the decision faced by Halsey appeared clear-cut. Rather than put undamaged ships at risk in the enemy's backyard by attempting to save a powerless hulk, he could recover the crew and sink the stricken cruiser, a procedure that was standard earlier in the war. Then he could proceed with his overall battle plan, which called for an end to air strikes against Formosa on 13 October. Instead, Halsey decided to tow the *Canberra* clear of the scene and cover the towing operation by conducting one more day of air strikes against Formosa.

Within ten minutes of the torpedo hit, the heavy cruiser *Wichita* had been alerted to take the *Canberra* in tow. Despite a heavy ground swell and gusting winds of up to 22 knots on the starboard beam, the two crews spent only twenty minutes rigging for tow in the dark. By the early hours of 14 October the *Wichita* was towing the *Canberra* in a southeasterly direction, making close to four knots. The remainder of McCain's task group deployed to the north to intercept any follow-up attacks the Japanese might have launched.

On board the *Houston* word spread about the decks that she would take the *Canberra*'s place in the screen of Task Group 38.1 as the point ship in the northwest sector of the formation. Most of the Japanese attacks were coming from the northwest.

A new day was dawning, but for at least one member of the *Houston*'s crew it was still Friday the thirteenth. Firecontrolman Third Class Joe Bob Lilius had already had two ships torpedoed out from under him, and he yearned for the stability that only dry land could provide. After the second torpedoing, he adjusted his watch and calendar to conform to Texas time.[4]

CHAPTER THREE

Torpedo!

The need to protect the *Canberra* towing operation upset Halsey's original plan to withdraw Task Force 38 to a fueling rendezvous during the night of 13–14 October. All task groups remained on station, and three of the four launched fighter sweeps against airfields on Formosa shortly after dawn.

By 1100 all the aircraft had been recovered. Task Force 38 began to move southward toward Luzon. The scuttlebutt on board the *Houston* had been correct. She had in fact been ordered to help restore the depleted cruiser strength of Task Group 38.1 and take the *Canberra's* spot in the screen. En route to McCain's task group, she sailed in company with the light carrier *Cabot* and the destroyers *Cowell* and *The Sullivans*—also detached from Task Group 38.2 but ordered to join the escort group then forming around the *Canberra*.

At 1544 the *Houston* left the other three ships close by the *Canberra* group and began maneuvering to take the exposed station no. 4060 in the Five Victor Five formation then maintained by McCain's group.

For topside watchstanders the brief look at the unlucky *Canberra* had been unsettling. The heavy cruiser still did not seem to be in serious danger of sinking, but she had become a near-stationary target, endangering her crew and those who were trying to assist her. Transformed suddenly from a prized asset to a serious liability to the task force, she was vulnerable to further battering both from the enemy and unforgiving sea.

The *Canberra*'s misfortune had a particularly strong impact on Captain Behrens of the *Houston*. He sought out his damage control officer, recently promoted Commander George Miller, on the after section of the bridge and asked him where the worst place to get torpedoed was. Miller had a ready answer. The *Houston*'s propulsion system was split into two independent units as a hedge against battle damage. The forward engine room and the forward fireroom, acting as one unit, drove the two outboard propellors; the after engine room and the after fireroom drove the two inboard ones. The ship would still have propellors turning on both the port and starboard sides if one of the independent propulsion units were to be knocked out.

The system had an Achilles' heel, however. Battle damage near the juncture of the forward engine room and the after fireroom could knock out both of the independent units. Furthermore, a torpedo hole the size of the *Canberra*'s could lead to massive flooding amidships and cause the ship to break in two.

The midships bulkhead at frame 79 separated the forward engine room and the after fireroom. According to Miller, it was the worst place the *Houston* could get hit. Behrens returned to the pilot house without comment.

Despite her exposed position in the formation, however, the *Houston* had little cause to feel like a sitting duck. In her first two night antiaircraft actions—the most difficult type to control—her defenses had been highly effective. There was a tight link between her combat information center, air defense officer, gunnery officer, 5-inch-gun directors, and air plot. An officer from the combat information center, manning the 5JP phone circuit, kept in direct contact with each of the other stations. He provided information from air and surface polar plots for station keeping and to determine clear sectors for firing. The air defense officer selected and designated the most threatening targets, assigning them either to the 5-inch-gun directors or to the automatic weapons, a decision that had to be approved by the gunnery officer, who maintained continuous contact with Captain Behrens. The 5-inch-gun directors, once they were trained along the reported bearings and searching in the reported range bands of approaching aircraft, would be coached into correct elevation settings by air plot. In every case this technique for reaching fire-control solutions worked. Japanese aircraft, even at low altitude, were being tracked from ranges of up to forty thousand yards by the *Houston*'s radar.

Full radar control of the *Houston*'s antiaircraft guns was used whenever possible, but there were exceptions. Her 6-inch main battery—with twelve guns in four turrets—was manned and ready to fire, but favorable opportunities had not yet presented themselves under the ship's 6-inch antiaircraft doctrine. Nevertheless, the directors for the main battery still tracked all bogeys reported by the combat information center. The 5-inch secondary battery mounts presented problems as well. There were recurring hydraulic failures, and three of the 5-inch mounts could not be operated in a fully automatic mode. Two were hand operated for elevation; one was hand operated to train its gun along the target bearing.

The 40mm and 20mm batteries were functioning almost perfectly. The only problem with them was their heavy reliance on tracers, which they needed to adjust their fire on rapidly moving targets. The solution was a long-term one—the development of a separate radar control system for the automatic weapons, or the 40mm guns at least. The gun crews would have to live with the probability that streams of their tracer rounds would continue to serve as beacons for enemy fliers at night.

Despite radar control and other improvements built into the antiaircraft capabilities of the *Houston*, the light cruiser, like her Asiatic Fleet predecessor, had faulty ammunition. Almost one-third of all the 5-inch ammunition was performing poorly. Many projectiles were prematurely detonating en route to their targets, and many failed to detonate altogether. In time the problem was found to lie with the 5-inch antiaircraft common ammunition, which used Mark 32 fuses. Most of these projectiles had been reenergized by the ship's force the preceding May. A routine test firing in September had first brought the problem to light, but an easy solution was precluded by three shortages: of time, of reenergizing materials, and of replacement ammunition. For the time being the *Houston* was stuck with what she had.

The marginally bad weather of the preceding few days still prevailed as the evening of 14 October approached. After the sun set the skies were still overcast, and visibility steadily decreased from the daytime limit of four miles. A choppy sea, driven by 30-knot winds from the northeast, was growing heavier.

Ashore, the Japanese were beginning to recover from the semiparalysis that had followed the raids on Okinawa and Formosa. At first the damage inflicted on Okinawan airfields had hindered their attempts to stage reinforcing aircraft through the Ryukyu Islands en route to Formosa, but by the afternoon of 14 October they had mustered enough aircraft to plan another major counterattack. On that day they decided to harass the *Canberra*'s towing group. The probes were very tentative, using few aircraft and seeming to lack organization. Most of the Japanese planes that had approached Task Force 38 were either shot down or driven away by the combat air patrol before they got within visual sighting range of the escort screen. The day's air activity had been incessant but had taken place far from the surface combatants. The *Houston*, in fact, had made only one visual contact all day, even though her radar operators were kept busy.

Early evening brought Japanese aircraft in larger groups of fifty or more. Something was different about these attack formations. Instead of being segregated by aircraft type, they were composed of curious mixtures. Americans with experience in earlier Pacific campaigns quickly noted as well that the technical performance of the aviators was not up to the previous standard of Japanese pilots. Their formation flying was ragged, giving the attacks as a whole a makeshift, almost ramshackle look. Perhaps the Japanese were finally scraping the bottom of the barrel, becoming critically short of both personnel and material assets.

This supposition seemed to be confirmed by a late-afternoon raid, which had been detected at 1630 coming in from the northwest at a range of more than one hundred miles. The American carriers launched their fighter interceptors, and by 1700 radar screens were showing tangled groups of dogfighting aircraft still forty miles distant from the nearest surface ships. The raid was smashed in less than an hour, and the remnants of the Japanese attack formation retreated toward the north and west. The carriers began to recover their fighter aircraft. The last plane landed at 1825, three minutes after sunset. Within five minutes, however, another group of Japanese aircraft suddenly appeared, closing from dead ahead at a range of twenty-five miles.

The attack developed rapidly. At a range of 18,000 yards the raiding force began to split up, just as it was taken under fire by the destroyer *Woodworth*, sailing somewhat apart from the main surface formation on picket duty to provide early warning of air attack. Moments later the *Woodworth* reported that the raid, minus three aircraft that had fallen prey to the destroyer's guns, was continuing toward Task Group 38.1.

The *Houston*'s fire control radars had locked on to the approaching raid by the time it crossed the horizon. At a range of 12,000 yards her forward 5-inch mounts opened fire, downing one attacker almost immediately. The gunners then shifted fire quickly to another aircraft, now in sight off the starboard bow.

Despite the poor light, all the Japanese aircraft—seven or eight Betty and Fran bombers—were now in sight. The *Houston*'s gunners squatted low in their mounts, attempting to silhouette the approaching aircraft against the lighter sky that rose above the deep-purple clouds on the horizon.[1]

Before long Japanese planes were swarming over the cruiser

from several directions close aboard. One aircraft flashed fore to aft along the port side, not more than fifty feet above the water. Automatic weapons battered it repeatedly until it crashed astern.

Meanwhile, the forward 5-inch guns were firing at their second target, which continued to close on the ship's starboard bow. Emerging from the darkness, the twin-engine Betty torpedo bomber continued to bore in toward the formation at an altitude of 150 feet. The forward 40mm and 20mm mounts on the starboard side took the plane under fire, hitting it repeatedly.

This new punishment from the *Houston*'s automatic weapons seemed only to attract the pilot's attention, however. Picking up the first tracers that sliced across the sky toward his aircraft, he turned directly toward the cruiser. At a distance of 1,500 yards he released a torpedo, then continued on an unwavering flight path across the cruiser's bow. He was hammered repeatedly by 40mm and 20mm fire until he crashed into the sea.

The *Houston* was getting hemmed in. Two other aircraft, also drawn by tracer fire, had approached from the port side. One launched a torpedo from the port quarter before falling victim to the cruiser's gunners. Another launched a torpedo from the port bow, then escaped into the night.

The cruiser was rolling heavily in the rough sea as she maneuvered at high speed to avoid the torpedoes. The two that had been launched from the planes on the port side passed her without doing harm. But the torpedo launched from the plane on her starboard side found its mark in a combination of circumstances that exceeded the gloomiest hypotheses of both Behrens and Miller.

The *Houston* was on a heavy roll to port, and her starboard side was exposed below the waterline. The torpedo struck near her bottom, midway between the centerline keel and the starboard bilge keel. A foot or two deeper and the torpedo might have passed under the ship without detonating. The difference between best case and worst case was a matter of inches. Since the hit was so far down, the full explosive force of the torpedo's warhead went straight into the hull and was fully absorbed by the ship.

The point of detonation was in the vicinity of frame 75, very close to the critical bulkhead that Miller had pointed out—the one at frame 79 that separated the forward engine room from the after fireroom. To make things worse, the ship's high maneuvering speed accentuated the destructive power of the sea, which was pouring into the *Houston*'s ruptured hull.

On the bridge, Lieutenant Commander Bill Kirkland, the special envoy from the city of Houston, felt the great ship being lifted in the water and twisted sideways. Then, while it settled back into the rough sea, it seemed to bounce. A series of low-frequency vibrations whipped the hull up and down the full length of the ship.[2]

Sailors at their battle stations topside saw a dull flash amidships from the ventilating blowers leading to the engine rooms, but there was no fire. A column of water rose from the starboard side. Steam poured from both smokestacks. The SK radar antenna assembly fell from its pedestal at the top of the foremast, and the after stay of the foremast carried away. A Kingfisher scout seaplane was knocked loose from its catapult on the main deck aft. It lay tilted at a 45-degree angle, with one bent wing resting against the crane on the hangar hatch cover.

Battle Station Helmsman H. M. Robertson had seen the torpedo from the lone Betty coming in from starboard. Expecting a hit, he wrapped his arms around the helm. The *Houston* rolled heavily to port. The explosion tore Robertson loose from the wheel, knocking him and several others all the way across the pilot house. As he picked himself up and returned to the helm, the ship began to lose way. All her propulsive power was gone.

Captain Behrens called down from the bridge above, asking if the *Houston* would answer the helm. The answer was no.[3]

The ship had lost all main electrical power. She was dark

and deathly quiet. The reassuring whine of the ventilation blowers and the sound of air rushing through the ducts ceased throughout the ship.

In air plot, far below the main deck, Lieutenant Julius Steuckert headed the team that had been manning the antiaircraft computers and the fire control switchboard, assisting directors no. 4 and 5 in controlling the 5-inch-gun mounts. Before long the rapid fire of the 40mm and 20mm mounts told them that at least one of the attacking aircraft had broken through the heavy 5-inch-gun fire.

Then a new noise came from below. It sounded like a slightly flattened marble rolling across the deck. Steuckert thought it might be a torpedo going underneath. He reported the sound to antiaircraft control. Everyone relaxed. At least that fish didn't have their name on it. But their reaction was premature.

Suddenly a torpedo struck. The floor plates in the air plot compartment slapped the soles of their feet, and their knees buckled from the upward thrust. The lights went out one row at a time as circuits failed. Battery-powered battle lanterns flickered on, weakly. The men were quiet, and the sounds of the ventilating system came to a halt.

Steuckert guessed that they had been torpedoed. On the other side of the bulkhead that separated air plot from the forward fireroom there was never any doubt. The compartment was flooding rapidly and would be filled within ten minutes. But that was enough time for all hands to escape and to secure the boilers by shutting valves from the third deck above. Steuckert and his men in air plot could hear the sounds of steam being shut down, and later the sounds of metal twisting as the fireroom flooded.

Just aft of the forward fireroom, the forward engine room had been opened to the sea by the hit. It flooded instantly. None of its occupants, including Commander Bill Potts, the chief engineer, escaped.

Bulkhead 79, the one that separated the forward engine room and the after fireroom, had been so severely torn and distorted by the explosion that flooding in the after fireroom was nearly instantaneous. In two minutes the compartment was completely filled with water.

In that time eighteen of the twenty-six men in the after fireroom had reached safety, even though two of them had been severely injured and would not live much longer. This miracle was a testament to selflessness and—in the case of Warrant Machinist Carl Behrend—to heroic self-sacrifice. For the men in the after fireroom the torpedo hit was crushing, breathtaking, unmistakable. They received two simultaneous yet distinct impressions. First, there was the sound of the torpedo's contact with the hull. Then came the noise and concussion of the explosion within the ship.

Ensign Don Smith, at his battle station as engineering officer of the watch, was standing between two boilers on the port side of the after fireroom's lower level. The force of the explosion thrust him upward about six inches. As he dropped back to the deck, he was aware of a shattering, crashing noise. He heard glass breaking and falling, then a sizzling sound. The lights had gone out. When, after a short delay, the battle lanterns came on, their weak light could barely pierce the cloud of thick, rusty-brown dust that hung in the motionless air. Then the lanterns went out, leaving them in total darkness.

Someone on the upper level shouted that steam was entering the compartment. Smith imagined the devastating effect of steam superheated to 825 degrees Fahrenheit. One lungful and you were gone. Soon it was evident that steam was not entering the compartment after all. But Smith could sense that flooding had begun. He told the men to clear out.[4]

The only exit from the lower level of the after fireroom was an escape trunk to the third deck. Superheater Burnerman B. C. Hall was one of the first ones into the trunk. As he followed a couple of others into it, he felt water rushing through the door. Behind him there was a jam.

At the moment of the explosion Warrant Machinist Carl Behrend, in charge of the upper level, had just returned from the starboard side, where he had been talking to a pair of checkmen, Water Tender Second Class Lloyd R. Blank and Water Tender First Class W. A. Dawkins. When the after fireroom went dark Behrend switched on his flashlight and dove for the vertical ladder that dropped to the escape trunk door on the lower level.

Two men who had been manning the boiler feed pumps, Fireman First Class Nolte V. Gause and Machinist Mate Second Class Claude E. Redford, followed Behrend down the ladder. Blank started down, but seeing the jam at the escape trunk, turned back. Along with Dawkins, he began to make his way to safety through an access hatch to the third deck that opened to the upper level of the after fireroom. By this time, Behrend had reached the door to the escape trunk. He stood beside it, holding his flashlight high and reassuring his shipmates.

Gause and Redford entered the trunk. At the top, where it flared out into a squarish chamber, several men were fumbling in the dark to undog the escape hatch to the third deck. The rest were strung along the ladder in a solid human column.

The cool water, covered with a layer of hot oil, had not yet risen to Behrend's shoulders when Redford entered the trunk, but in a second it was over Behrend's head. At that instant the hatch at the top of the trunk came open, and the built-up air pressure escaped. The trunk immediately filled with water.

Behrend was trapped by rising water before he could enter the trunk. He saved his shipmates by passing up the chance to save himself. He would receive a posthumous award of the Navy Cross.

On the third deck, Chief Water Tender Robert L. Stein had charge of a repair party in the compartment directly over the escape trunk leading from the after fireroom. Wearing a head lantern, Stein had just begun to work on the escape hatch when it was pushed open from below.

Stein could see that congestion in the flared portion of the trunk was blocking upward movement. He began to pull out one man after another, passing them back to his repair party.

The first three came out in good shape, without any oil on them. The next four were covered with it. By this time water was gushing up through the hatch, then draining back down again when the ship rolled.

Stein groped in the oily water. He grabbed at an arm, lost it, then caught it again. He brought out Water Tender First Class R. M. Cranford, then Fireman Second Class C. J. Freehouse, then Fireman First Class J. R. Cox, all of them losing consciousness. Freehouse had been assigned to the no. 3 boiler, which was located on the starboard side from which virtually no one would be saved. He probably owed his life to the occasional need to check thermometers near the ship's centerline; this had left him close enough to the escape trunk when the torpedo struck.

Next out, miraculously unhurt, was Gause. But Redford, the last man in the human column, had been underwater for at least a minute at the bottom of the escape trunk. He had swallowed a lot of water and was having trouble breathing.

Stein held the hatch open for three or four more minutes, watching and reaching. There was a lot of water entering his compartment, and the pressure was great enough on a port roll of the ship to force any remaining bodies out of the escape trunk. Stein reluctantly concluded that further rescue was unlikely. He finally dogged down the escape hatch and began to assist the injured.

Two of the men rescued from the escape trunk, Cranford and Cox, were suffering from severe respiratory distress. The ship's head laundryman, Coxswain Jacob Mein, spread clothing about the deck to provide footing for members of the repair party who were trying to revive them through artificial respiration. Oily water sloshed heavily through the compartment.

Cranford never regained consciousness, and was eventually pronounced dead by one of the ship's doctors. Undaunted, Cranford's shipmates carried him topside and worked on him for another hour before they finally admitted to themselves that they could not bring him back.

It soon became evident that Cox, who was suffering from internal injuries, could not stand the pressure of artificial respiration. He was taken topside and treated by Dr. Fred Ruoff before being moved to an emergency sick bay. There, despite careful nursing, he died within a few hours.

The other two sailors who appeared to be in the greatest difficulty, Freehouse and Redford, both recovered rapidly.

In addition to Blank and Dawkins, five others had attempted to escape directly from the upper level, through the main access hatch to the third deck on the starboard side. Before the explosion Chief Electrician's Mate Adee Martin was being assisted by four men on the distribution board and the switchboard from the catwalk on the upper level of the after fireroom. Machinist's Mate Second Class Paul Jamsky and Machinist's Mate First Class Allen Hayslett were assigned as generator men, while Electrician's Mate Second Class Frank Sears helped Martin at the distribution board and Electrician's Mate Third Class Roland Grass manned the phones.

Hayslett and Grass were sitting on the catwalk, leaning against the switchboard at the time of the explosion. Hayslett, thrown upward, struck his head before landing on his right side. This resulted in a concussion, two broken vertebrae, and a smashed elbow. Grass was lying nearby, motionless, entangled in a mass of telephone wires and twisted steel.

Immediately after the explosion, just before the lights went out, Martin glimpsed Sears running toward a ladder on the port side. This was an indirect route to an escape hatch on the lower level that Sears had apparently mapped out in advance. That was the last Martin ever saw of Sears, who may have fallen through a dislodged grating and lost his chance to escape.

Martin found a flashlight and checked out the companionway leading to an upper-level access hatch about fifteen feet away. Despite some missing gratings the path was clear.

By this time Jamsky and Dawkins had already reached the hatch and were undogging it. Blank was standing by. Hayslett and Grass were still stretched out on the companionway. Martin first reached Hayslett, who regained consciousness as Martin began to pull him to his feet. Grass, meanwhile, was trying without luck to pull himself to his knees. Martin yanked Grass free of the phone wires and other weight that had been pinning him down. Grass scrambled through the escape hatch and emerged at the second deck scuttle.

Hayslett, however, still could not walk. As water and oil began to rise over the gratings of the catwalk, Martin dragged him to the ladder and tried to lift him to the open escape hatch. Martin, with a badly strained back, lacked the strength. Leaving Hayslett propped against the ladder, Martin climbed upward for help and managed to catch up with Blank before he disappeared through the scuttle above. Meanwhile, Hayslett started up the ladder himself, using only his left arm and left leg. He stayed just above the water level of the rapidly flooding compartment. Each time the water reached his knees, he managed to pull himself up one more rung. Finally, Blank reappeared and pulled Hayslett free of the water that had finally risen above his waist.

Hayslett was the last man to leave the after fireroom alive. Eight shipmates, including the heroic Behrend, remained below as the steadily thickening layer of compressed brown dust finally gave way to the sea.

In addition to the four major engineering spaces, one other large compartment suffered severe damage from the torpedo hit. The machine shop on the starboard side of the third deck stretched directly over the forward engine room, between frames 69 and 79, and lay adjacent to the evaporator room, which ran along the centerline of the ship for the same distance fore and aft.

Just prior to the explosion, four men were at their stations in the machine shop, two were in the evaporator room, and nine relief men and repair party members were in the starboard side passageway.

The force of the explosion in the forward engine room separated the low-pressure turbine from the reduction gear, blowing it upward with enough force to open two seams in the armored third deck. The case-hardened steel deck plates were lifted a good six inches. Almost instantly a jet of superheated steam shot through the machine shop. The door to the evaporator room warped, and the bulkhead was badly crumpled.

The sailors in the passageway, seated or lying on the deck in accordance with general quarters procedure, were thrown upward about three feet. They were the only men to escape from the area of the machine shop, and one of them succumbed to severe burns about thirty-six hours later. Neither the four men trapped in the machine shop nor the two others caught in the evaporator room got out of their compartments in time.

The men in the passageway just forward of the ruptured seam in the armored deck all received burns. Fireman First Class Les Quay had a routine assignment in the forward engine room, but his battle station was with the no. 1 repair party near the machine shop. When general quarters sounded that evening, Quay had left the engine room with some of his repair gang and dogged down the hatch to the machine shop above—for the last time, as things turned out.

Quay and his mates were accustomed to spending long hours at general quarters. They were conversing in a relaxed way when they heard a mount directly over them begin to fire. The force of the explosion fractured Quay's leg and knocked him out. He came to and heard sailors nearby yelling for everyone to get out of the area. He was still trying to crawl through the darkness and debris when a search party found him and began to pull him free. He was hauled through an escape scuttle overhead and taken topside through the after mess deck.[5]

The machine shop compartment was abandoned to complete flooding.

High above these desperate scenes, on the darkened bridge, an air of calm still prevailed as the captain fought grimly to regain control of his stricken ship. But the initial reports coming up to the bridge were ominous.

CHAPTER FOUR

"Abandon Ship"

Captain Behrens's task of regaining control of the stricken *Houston* was complicated by the fact that the torpedo explosion had put most of the ship's internal communications networks out of action. What little telephone capability survived the hull-wrenching blast was soon fading away. The voices of the phone talkers grew fainter; one final outburst carried over their bridge circuit: "What the hell's going on up there?!"[1]

The question, from the emergency after steering compartment, hung in the air.

For the time being, any question of emergency steering control was academic. The *Houston* lay dead in the water. She was heeling over to starboard, coming closer and closer to capsizing, while the main engineering compartments continued to fill with seawater. Her main deck was awash on the starboard side. This compounded the problem of flooding below decks; water from the main deck continued to cascade through distorted hatches, ladder wells, and ventilation ducts down to the spaces below.

The captain had lost contact with his damage control central station—below the third deck forward—immediately after the torpedo hit, but news of the uncontrolled flooding quickly reached the bridge by word of mouth. In the major engineering

spaces, after the first ten minutes, only the men in the after engine room still seemed to have a chance of saving their compartment, which was flooding through the inboard end of the
stern tube and around the bulkhead stuffing gland for the no. 1
shaft. Both of these dangerous leaks started when the torpedo
blast broke the coupling of the reduction gear, causing the
shaft—pulled by propellor drag—to slip aft by two and a
half feet.

To fight the flooding, damage control teams rigged three
relatively small submersible pumps through an escape scuttle.
Their power was supplied by the after auxiliary emergency
generator. The first pump was working within eleven minutes
of the hit, the others soon after. Even with all three pumps in
operation, however, the water continued to rise rapidly in the
after engine room. After twenty minutes the space had to be
abandoned. Damage control personnel were able to retrieve
two of the three pumps.

Flooding on the third deck, above the four engineering
spaces, was also extensive. As the ship settled deeper, water
from below flowed freely through the opened seams of the armored deck. Distortions in bulkheads and watertight door
frames, created by the blast, made it impossible to seal off
third-deck compartments, and the flooding continued to spread
until it covered that deck completely between bulkheads 38
and 101, a length of 252 feet.

Relatively shallow flooding reached as high as the second
deck, posing a threat to five spaces and adding to the problem
of the *Houston*'s stability, which was most endangered in the
first minutes after the hit. The only way that damage control
parties could gain access to some of these second-deck compartments was to open hatches from the main deck, much of
which was awash. This complicated their task by admitting
still more water to the second deck.

The *Houston* had fallen far astern of her task group's battle
formation, which continued to steam at 25 knots or better. Captain Behrens had to signal his predicament to the task group

commander, but his radios were out and the chances of visual contact grew more remote with each passing minute.

Responding to orders from the bridge, Signalman First Class Al Ciampi attempted to contact the signal bridge of the carrier *Wasp* with a hand-held blinker light powered by batteries. His effort was hampered by the cloudy night as well as the steadily increasing distance between the ships. The *Wasp* did not respond. Ciampi tried again, working the blinker in desperation, signaling that he had an urgent message to send.

The minutes seemed like hours. Finally, the *Wasp* blinked back: PROCEED WITH YOUR MESSAGE.[2]

News of the *Houston*'s plight was relayed quickly to the task group commander, Vice Admiral McCain. His response on the TBS (talk between ships) tactical radio net was immediate: "*Boyd, Cowell, Grayson*—stand by *Houston*."

The three destroyers hauled out of the task group formation and raced toward the *Houston*, drifting dead in the water, in imminent danger of capsizing. Their radarscopes showed that several Japanese aircraft were still in the vicinity.[3] As the stricken cruiser settled into the trough of a heavy sea, her rolling increased. They were long, painful rolls, and they were growing heavier.

In damage control central, Commander Miller directed his phone talker, Yeoman Third Class Hank Shafman, to check out the stations on the 2JZ sound-powered telephone network. Even though the ship's service telephones had failed within the first minute after the torpedo hit, breaking his contact with the bridge, Miller found that the 2JZ circuit remained intact. Shafman could talk with all five repair stations and with the after engine room, until rapid flooding forced the abandonment of that space. Main engine control, located in the forward engine room, had been knocked off the network at the instant the torpedo exploded. There was a lot of excited chattering on the net, and Shafman appreciated the relative coolness of the talker at repair 5, who always used the correct procedure to capture the net when he had a priority message to send.[4]

With his phone links to the bridge destroyed, Commander Miller began the fight to save his ship in relative isolation below the armored deck. Based on his assumption that the torpedo hit amidships would result in the flooding of all four major engineering spaces, his initial calculations told him that the *Houston* would be taking on board more than five thousand tons of seawater—half of her total displacement. No ship had ever survived such massive flooding.

To make things worse, the *Houston* had already suffered from a minor stability problem before she was torpedoed. The change in Halsey's battle plan that had been caused by the *Canberra*'s being torpedoed had kept the *Houston* from making a scheduled fueling rendezvous, and her empty fuel tanks caused her to ride higher in the water than she otherwise would have at the time of the hit. With thousands of tons of floodwater already in the ship, however, it was too late to ballast her down by filling the empty tanks with seawater.

The worst threat to stability for the moment was coming from the free surface water that surged from side to side in the rapidly flooding engineering spaces. This, together with the green water washing over the main deck on the starboard side, had the potential of bringing any severe roll the ship might normally take in bad weather past the point of no return.

In the first few minutes after the torpedo hit, nothing could be done to ease the stability crisis. The ship would have to save herself until damage control measures could be taken. With each roll to starboard Miller found himself keeping a close watch on the inclinometer, which gauged the *Houston*'s degree of list. His first priority would have to be preventing the ship from capsizing.

The needle swung steadily toward the capsize point, which Miller had calculated to be a 41-degree roll. He could feel the ship shuddering, and could hear her groaning from the unaccustomed strain amidships as the needle passed 37 degrees. An extra gust of wind or a slightly larger wave at this point and it would all be over. Finally the needle started back. In a few moments Miller would begin a new vigil with the next terrible roll.

Eventually, with the ship settling deeper into the water, the severity of the rolls began to decrease and the inclinometer registered 20 degrees. The *Houston*'s starboard list steadied at around 16. With this first crisis over, Miller ordered his damage control central crew to a secondary damage control station on the second deck, directly above.

Even as the danger of capsizing was apparently passing, a new problem was created by the rapidly growing weight of floodwater amidships. With buoyancy left only at the bow and stern, the *Houston* had developed a dangerous sag in the middle. It threatened to buckle the keel and the main longitudinal strength beams and break the ship in half, snapping stem and stern together with the awful suddenness of a book being slammed shut.

The crew could hear the terrible sound of the ship working against herself amidships as an ominous torque developed between her forward and after halves. The great longitudinals, massive steel beams running fore and aft below the main deck, were buckling in several places. Rivets, under great pressure, popped loose from beams and bulkheads with the sharp crack of pistol shots and whizzed through the air with lethal velocity. The transverse bulkheads of the flooding compartments began to give way to the steadily increasing pressure of the sea.

On the bridge Captain Behrens had received reports that the keel was probably broken, that progressive flooding was still unchecked after the abandonment of the after engine room, and that the ship could probably not withstand a tow to safety of over one thousand miles.

At that point Commander W. V. Pratt III brought the destroyer *Grayson* close aboard on the *Houston*'s starboard quarter. A message from McCain was flashed over: IF *HOUSTON* REQUIRES A TOW, *BOSTON* IS READY. The reply flickered back from the *Houston*'s hand-held blinker: TOW NOT REQUIRED. SHIP APPEARS TO BE BREAKING UP.

After relaying the message back to McCain, who had begun maneuvering his task group to remain within TBS broadcast range, the *Grayson* stood by for further word from the *Houston*. It was not long in coming: AM ABANDONING SHIP.[5]

Behrens went to the wing of the bridge and gave his instructions to all within earshot: "This is the captain speaking. My order now is for you to abandon ship, wear your life jackets, hang together with the floater nets and rafts, and you will be picked up by destroyers."[6]

It was about 2030, less than two hours from the time of the torpedo hit. All stations below the third deck had already been abandoned, except where damage control and rescue parties still labored and, in after steering, where men still struggled unsuccessfully to get the jammed rudder back amidships, using their own muscles instead of electrical power.

Miller had reestablished his damage control headquarters on the second deck by this time. He called together his leading assistants: Lieutenants Joe Simpson, Charlie York, and Rives Brown; and Chief Carpenter Les Schnable. They had been working throughout the ship to control flooding on the third deck and below.

As the group assembled word arrived that Captain Behrens had given the order to abandon ship. Miller called for an assessment of the ship's condition. The picture was not encouraging. Progressive flooding continued as the ship settled deeper into the water. Repair parties would no sooner shore up one bulkhead than another would start to buckle. The ship was still listing badly, even though the danger of capsizing had lessened. And there was absolutely no hope of restoring propulsion or main electrical power.

Miller probed his assistants for more positive news. No one spoke. Finally, Carpenter Schnable broke the awkward silence, pointing out that at least the ship was still afloat.

Conditions had, in fact, stabilized somewhat. The groaning from the *Houston*'s innards subsided. Given the chance, the crew might be able to control the flooding. With any luck, they could probably get the ship through the night. And if they did have to abandon ship, it would be far better to leave her in daylight. Miller started topside in hopes of getting the captain to halt the abandonment. After a few minutes, he reached the bridge and presented his case to Behrens. The captain did not agree.

Meanwhile, Lieutenant Commander Kirkland carried the abandon-ship order from the bridge to Commander Clarence Broussard, the ship's executive officer, who was at his battle station on the fantail. Broussard questioned the order; he believed the ship would stay afloat. Kirkland advised Broussard to tell the captain so. Broussard would have a closer look first. Accompanied by a volunteer, Yeoman Second Class Douglas Drysdale, he began his own inspection of the critical areas below decks.

As abandon-ship activity got under way, Behrens contacted the destroyer *Cowell* and requested that she come alongside to take off some of the *Houston*'s crew. Weather and sea conditions were not favorable for such a transfer—they duplicated a mariner's worst nightmares. The *Houston* was lying broadside to a stiff northeasterly wind, making considerable leeway to starboard as she rolled violently in the trough of a heavy sea. The crippled cruiser had a severe list to starboard. Visibility was poor. Japanese aircraft flew overhead.

Defying these conditions, Commander C. W. Parker brought the *Cowell* in for a valiant approach to the *Houston*'s port side, which was riding high. Men in life jackets were already bobbing in the oily sea. Others leaped from the *Houston* as the two ships rolled toward each other; some of them landed on top of sailors working on the *Cowell*'s main deck. Still others, who jumped when the two ships had rolled apart and were separated by fifteen to twenty feet of open water, fell between them to an unknown end; their screams and mute evidence on the *Houston*'s hull the next morning indicated that their fate had been cruel indeed.[8] Officers from the *Houston* began to move around the main deck to prevent men from jumping directly onto the destroyer.

On one converging roll the ships collided with a fearsome

impact that caused some of the *Houston*'s crew below decks to believe that they had been torpedoed again. The *Cowell* suffered significant damage to her superstructure and was quickly told to lie off close aboard.

Whenever Japanese aircraft reappeared, they were taken under fire by the destroyers. From time to time shrapnel rained down on the *Houston*'s main deck and the crew had to seek cover. One of the Japanese bombers came close enough to launch a torpedo, but it missed and ran between the *Houston* and the *Grayson*.

In order to tow men in the water toward the destroyers, the *Houston* attempted to lower her own motor whaleboats into the heavy sea. The severe list to starboard made it impossible to swing the no. 2 boat clear of the port side, so a six-man detail from the main deck aft, under Chief Boatswain's Mate Chuck O'Connor, manned the no. 1 boat on the starboard side. Their first attempts to lower the boat in standard fashion, with her crew on board, were thwarted by malfunctioning starboard boat falls and generally hazardous conditions. The seas eventually smashed the boat into the boat-deck ladder, breaking O'Connor's hip. The craft had to be lowered empty. The five remaining crewmen ran forward, jumped over the side of the *Houston*, and swam aft to climb into the boat.

Next the crew rigged a steering oar, but it had little effect in the heavy sea. Their attempts to maintain course by periodically reversing engines were equally unsuccessful. Finally they were ordered back on board the *Houston* after a fruitless attempt to locate life rafts in the darkness. With only a little power and virtually no steering capability, the boat they were riding was hardly more than a life raft itself.

This became evident when the *Houston* tried to recover the boat, a task nearly as hazardous as her launching. The crew managed with great difficulty to bring her alongside and to catch a heaving line and make it fast to the bow. As the boat was pulled in, the seas began dashing her against the *Houston*'s anchor. Four of the crew exited by climbing up the paravane chains used for minesweeping; the fifth man was hauled back on board the cruiser with a manila line.

Next there was an attempt to pull the boat around the *Houston*'s bow to the cruiser's windward side, and from there to trail her astern. But a heavy swell swept her against the ship's anchor. The craft, rapidly filling with water and beyond hope of recovery, was cast off with a crushed side.[9]

The failure of the courageous attempt at small-boat rescue was practically preordained. Driven by the stiff wind, the *Houston* was making leeway toward the southwest faster than the rafts, the net loads, and the individually drifting sailors, who were being strung out to windward. The *Grayson* soon parted company with the two other destroyers and began to look for survivors along the track that the *Houston* was leaving in her portside wake.

The painstaking search by all three destroyers would continue into the daylight hours. They showed a cautious bit of searchlight whenever they were alerted by whistles or cries from the sea, but they were extremely wary about illuminating targets for the Japanese aircraft still in the area. Large groups from the *Houston*, clinging to rafts or nets, were generally the first men to be found. Individuals who had been separated from others were much harder for the destroyers' lookouts to spot. Some men undoubtedly paid with their lives for going it alone in violation of basic survival procedure. The *Grayson* eventually rescued 176 of the *Houston*'s crew, and the *Cowell* was credited with 195 rescues. The *Boyd*—remaining close aboard to serve as a communications relay for the *Houston*— recovered 380, which surpassed the number of her own crew. All of the *Houston* men thus recovered were subsequently transferred to larger ships.

While the destroyers continued their search and rescue operations, abandonment of the *Houston* proceeded in a relatively quiet, orderly manner. A few men who tried to go over the starboard side quickly learned that in only a few seconds the speed and direction of the *Houston*'s drift took them right back to the ship's main deck, which was still awash on that side.

Most proceeded directly to the port side. Seaman First Class Anthony Caserta had been bounced roughly about his battle station in director no. 1 by the shock of the torpedo hit. Limping badly, but not yet feeling the pain, he was hustled down to the main deck by Boatswain's Mate First Class Francis Steenberg, who had been in charge of the director. Steenberg had survived the torpedoing of the cruiser *Helena*, and Caserta relied upon his experience. When they reached the main deck, Steenberg pushed Caserta over the port side. As soon as he hit the dark sea Caserta felt his injured leg start to burn like fire. The oil in the water was bad for his wound, but it occurred to him that the salt might help stop the heavy bleeding.

Steenberg jumped into the water behind Caserta. Neither man had a life jacket, but both were good swimmers. Together they swam from raft to raft, looking for friends at first but finally, as they began to tire, picking one raft and clinging to it.

They drifted for several hours before they were sighted and approached by the *Boyd*. Men from the raft began climbing up a cargo net that had been draped over the destroyer's side. Steenberg grabbed the net first, urging Caserta to follow suit. Just then the *Boyd* began to roll toward the two men, dipping the net deeper into the water. In a few moments, she rolled back the other way, breaking the net free of the water. Steenberg was gone. Caserta was recovered by the *Boyd* minutes later.[10]

As this incident suggests, getting to the rescuing destroyers proved to be a harrowing experience. Sergeant Byron Harris of the *Houston*'s marine detachment certainly wouldn't deny it. Harris was a 20mm gunner heading a four-man crew that manned one of the portside mounts. The gun crew felt the *Houston* rise, then fall about twenty-five feet deeper into the water. As she recovered from the drop, the port side rose higher and higher until the main deck was awash on the starboard side. Harris was certain the ship would capsize.

When word was passed about the main deck, Harris moved

toward his assigned abandon-ship station on the starboard side; on the way he was diverted to a Jacob's ladder on the port side, back near the mount he had manned. Once in the water, he tried to swim to a nearby destroyer, but the ship was upstream and the current was too strong to battle. Harris and a friend, Private First Class William Redd, saw the *Houston* quickly drifting away. Soon it left them alone in the darkness. They blew their survival whistles in hopes of alerting an unseen destroyer, but without success. To reduce the weight and drag on their life jackets, they kicked off their field shoes. The minutes passed, and they grew weak from seasickness and the oil and salt water they had swallowed. Finally they drifted into the vicinity of an eight-man life raft with a lone sailor on board. As other survivors emerged from the darkness, they were pulled on to the raft until it became hopelessly overloaded. The healthier men left the raft to make way for the sick and injured.

The commanding officer of the marine detachment, Captain J. C. O'Connor, drifted into view and was hauled on board. He organized an attempt to paddle the raft, but the effort had little effect in the heavy seas. To Harris the overloaded raft looked like a drunken roller coaster on rubber rails. It came close to capsizing time after time.

The sole illumination came from exploding shells. Concussions from ordnance exploding underwater knocked the wind out of the floating men. Shrapnel rained into the water around Harris and the others, but the rough seas gave them the equivalent of foxhole protection, and no one was wounded.

Around midnight a destroyer loomed suddenly out of the darkness and nearly hit the raft as she sped into the night without sighting or hearing the shouting survivors. The destroyer's wake almost capsized the raft; the men in the water had to right it and move the weaker ones back toward the center.

Harris saw an occasional ship in the distance turn on her searchlights to look for survivors. This invariably drew more Japanese aircraft.

At about 0430, after the men had been in the water for

roughly eight hours, the *Grayson* suddenly appeared. A lookout sighted the raft at the last moment, and the destroyer reversed engines hurriedly to keep from hitting it. The newly created suction capsized the raft and pulled Harris, who had been swimming alongside, under the water. His life jacket, which had been absorbing water for hours, had reached the saturation point. Harris was unable to get his head above the surface of the water. He swallowed oily water and began to pass into oblivion.

Hours later, Harris opened his eyes on board the *Grayson*. His only memory, a vague one, had been of someone untying a line from around his body. They had pumped the water out of him and removed his oil-soaked clothing. He was lying in a bunk. A mess steward was asking if he would like something to eat.

Despite severe overcrowding on all the destroyers, the crews managed to clean up the oil-soaked men pulled from the sea. The wounded were treated with what modest medical supplies were available, and they were provided fresh clothing from the ships' stores and crews. Perhaps the most difficult problem was finding the survivors places to sleep. The destroyermen soon learned to relieve their watchstanders by sending each man after his own relief. Otherwise the temporarily empty rack or hammock would soon be occupied by an exhausted refugee from the *Houston*.

The lack of sleeping space was not an obstacle to the more imaginative members of the *Houston*'s crew, however. Firecontrolman Third Class Jim Potter, while he was a guest of the *Boyd*, slept among other places on torpedo tubes, on the searchlight platform, and in after steering.[11]

Leaving the crippled ship proved difficult for men who started out healthy, but it was much riskier for men who had been injured by the torpedo blast and its effects. The difficulty of launching the motor whaleboat had dashed all hopes of using that means of transferring the wounded, so those who did leave were to a great extent on their own.

After Les Quay had been pulled from the machine shop, his burns were bandaged and he was brought to the main deck. As he lay there, he heard the sounds of the *Cowell*'s attempt to come alongside. Officers were telling sailors not to make the hazardous leap to the destroyer's deck. There were occasional screams. Quay felt the great jolt when the two ships banged together and heard the captain on the bridge above, ordering the destroyer to lay off.

When his shipmates prepared to abandon ship, Quay did not want to go, but the others were adamant about his coming with them. Quay joined a group going over the port side and was eventually helped into one of the rafts. Two destroyers passed close by without stopping. A third one spotted the raft, approached cautiously, and lowered a cargo net. The *Houston* sailors lashed the raft to the net and climbed aboard the ship. But Quay could not move. Destroyermen scrambled down the net with a stretcher, lashed Quay onto it, and hoisted him aboard.

In sick bay, the medical personnel did not have the proper means to set Quay's broken ankle or clean his burns. They gave him painkilling shots until he could be transferred to the cruiser *Santa Fe* the following day.[12]

Some of the *Houston*'s wounded had received head injuries. Seaman First Class Jim Bledsoe had found Joe Bob Lilius wandering about the main deck in a state of total confusion. He did not recognize anyone; he did not understand anything; he had no memory. Lilius clearly could not be left alone, so Bledsoe kept him by his side when he abandoned ship a short while later.[13]

As the evening wore on, it became evident that a sizeable portion of the crew was not ready to leave the *Houston*. Some, in the damage control and rescue parties, had been too busy to think about abandoning ship. Others were made hesitant by the sight of men struggling in the treacherous seas. Still others were too severely injured to go over the side.

The reasons for their reluctance to obey the abandon-ship

order were many and varied, but almost all of the remaining men had one thing in common that kept them on board, and that was the hope—which grew into a conviction as the hours went by—that the *Houston* would remain afloat.

CHAPTER FIVE

Turnabout

Even as they continued preparations to abandon ship, some of the *Houston*'s crew found themselves helping their shipmates back on board.

Signalman First Class John Rooney, the supervisor of the signal bridge, had among other responsibilities that of disposing of classified codebooks. After hearing the order to abandon ship, he placed the books in weighted canvas bags that he had fashioned earlier, when he served as a bunting repairman. He left the signal bridge for the main deck, where he could drop the classified material over the side. During the abandon-ship procedure he was to act as signalman for the marine detachment, so he went aft to his station. No one was there. This suited Rooney, who by now had decided that he didn't want to leave the ship yet. He walked about the main deck and soon heard loud voices coming from the port side. Men in the water were calling for help. Rooney and several others broke into the boatswain's locker nearby with a fire axe. They found lines that could be lowered into the water.

Rooney returned to the signal bridge, where most of the watch was still assembled. Before long Commander Broussard appeared, on his way to see Captain Behrens. He felt that the ship could be saved, and he needed communicators to keep the *Houston* in touch with any assisting ships. To a man, the communicators agreed to stay on board.[1]

Electrician's Mate Second Class Frank Campanella had been assigned to a damage control party on the second deck, starboard side. When the order to abandon ship came down, he sent the other two members of his party topside. Then he went to the port side to determine the situation there.

Campanella ran into another repair crew carrying handy-billy pumps down the escape hatch to the after engine room. The crew was headed by Ensign Robert Rock. Campanella took a pump and climbed into the flooded compartment. Flashing a battle lantern on the bulkhead that separated the after engine room from the after fireroom, Campanella could see the uncontrolled seepage around the propellor shaft. The pumps were not keeping up. The flooding continued to worsen, and he and the others finally had to abandon the compartment.

Campanella returned topside and went to the fantail. It was deserted at the time, but he soon heard cries for help coming from the water. Some sailors who had left the ship earlier were trying to come back on board from the starboard side. Campanella reached the nearest man with his outstretched hand when the ship rolled to starboard and pulled him back on board without difficulty. Then the two of them began to pull others in.

A while later, when the *Cowell* was coming alongside, Campanella had to restrain a young sailor trying to make the hazardous jump to the main deck of the violently rolling destroyer. The young man broke down, wrapped his arms around his rescuer's neck, and began to cry. He did not leave Campanella's side for the next few days.[2]

Electrician's Mate First Class Allen Hayslett had been treated for a back injury and brought up to the main deck after his escape from the after fireroom. A sedative had been administered to him, but the severe pain in his back had not subsided. Helpless, he watched the men work, quietly and with a surprising absence of confusion, given the circumstances. Life rafts and nets were lowered into the sea, and individuals climbed down lines and nets to rescue the stranded. Japanese aircraft still flew by intermittently, and shrapnel from the stiff antiaircraft fire that greeted the planes occasionally rained down on the *Houston*'s weather decks, sending all hands not already protected to seek cover.

Hayslett was just about resigned to his near-hopeless situation when Ensign Don Smith from the after fireroom appeared at his side. Smith had a bowl of ice cubes to ease Hayslett's thirst and a bottle of brandy to ease his pain.[3]

Commander Charles Cook, the navigator, had left the bridge to take a walk around the main deck about a half hour after the abandon-ship order had been given. The forecastle appeared to be clear, but for some reason a number of men were still gathered on the main deck aft. He approached on the port side and found a full division of men drawn up in two ranks, waiting quietly. No one seemed to be in a great hurry to go over the side, for the ship's stability continued to improve. Cook continued on his way aft. As he reached the fantail, he heard Lieutenant Steuckert's voice, with a ring of authority, pass the word not to abandon ship. Several cheers rose from the darkness.[4]

Commander Broussard's inspection strengthened his conviction that the *Houston* could be kept afloat, at least for the rest of the night. His opinion was reinforced by Commander Miller, who had returned to the bridge to persuade the captain to rescind the abandon-ship order. After Miller and Broussard had conferred, the latter presented a convincing case in a few moments of urgent discussion with Behrens.

The *Houston*'s blinker flashed out the message for relay to McCain: FLOODING UNDER CONTROL. HAVE CEASED ABANDONING. REQUEST *BOSTON* TAKE *HOUSTON* IN TOW.[5]

Approval of the request came quickly. Within twenty minutes the heavy cruiser *Boston* approached and maneuvered to pass the towing cable. Miller rushed from the bridge to the forecastle to supervise the rigging. He was relieved: The remarkable turnabout had given the crew a fighting chance to save the ship. Their experience had been like going halfway down Niagara Falls in a barrel, then reversing course to get back to the top again.

But with relief came more apprehension. Getting the *Houston* through the night was one thing; getting her back to Ulithi was something else. The odds were definitely against a successful tow, and Miller had put himself squarely on record by urging the captain and the executive officer to buck the odds. Miller had just volunteered for a formidable task under wartime conditions that could make even the simplest tasks devilishly difficult to carry out. A sneering monkey had leaped on his back to mock him at every turn. The monkey would stay there for the best part of a year.

When he reached the forecastle Miller confronted the first of many problems he would face in his effort to save the ship. On his way up to the bridge, he had left orders with the forecastle crew to stand by to rig for a tow. Upon his return, however, the forecastle was virtually deserted. Nearly two-thirds of the crew had obeyed the order to abandon ship before it was rescinded. Most of the deckhands with experience on the forecastle had already gone over the side.

Miller began to despair when out of the darkness Lieutenant Julius Steuckert appeared, cheerfully reporting for duty. Steuckert had been one of Miller's damage control assistants before his assignment to antiaircraft plot. With his radars made inoperative by the total loss of electrical power, he was ready to return to Miller's side.

Miller's first concern was to get his damage control people to assemble an untrained crew of volunteers for hazardous and unfamiliar work. Then, in the dark, he had to find the towing gear as well as a crew capable of heaving the *Boston*'s towing cable in and shackling it to the *Houston*'s anchor chain. They would pay out the heavy chain by gradually releasing the brake on the anchor windlass, which, lacking power, had been useless for heaving in the cable. All of this would have to be done in the dark, on a slippery and rolling deck, in the steady rain that was beginning to fall, and under continuous Japanese air attack. The monkey on Miller's back began to snicker.

The *Boston* approached flying the flag of a cruiser division commander who knew that the *Canberra* and the *Wichita* had rigged their tow in twenty minutes. He would be anxious to repeat their performance. But the wind and sea conditions did not look promising for the effort. The *Boston* had originally been rigged to pass the towline from her starboard quarter. With the wind blowing from port to starboard, the *Boston* would normally have taken station on the windward side of the *Houston*. The *Boston*, however, was riding much higher in the water than the *Houston* and therefore had a substantially faster rate of drift. If she tried to maintain station to windward during the tow, she would be in constant danger of drifting down on the crippled cruiser and perhaps colliding with her. If the *Boston* took station in the *Houston*'s lee and rerigged the tow from her port side, the direction of the wind and her faster rate of drift might actually assist somewhat in the towing process.

The drawback of this new arrangement was that Miller's makeshift forecastle crew had to heave harder and longer to bring on board the *Boston*'s towing cable while the wind pushed their tow ship farther away from them. Urged on by exhortations to heave for their lives, the *Houston* sailors brought in the heavy manila lead line inch by inch, until the eye of the heavy steel towing cable finally appeared.

A heavy U-shaped shackle would be used to bend the cable onto the *Houston*'s anchor chain, forming the crucial junction in the towing rig. The shackle had a large, removable bolt held in place by a relatively small steel retaining pin, which had become the object of a hectic search by Miller and others. As they groped through unfamiliar gear lockers, the pin might as well have been a needle.

The search continued, and flashing light messages from the

Boston revealed mounting impatience. The heavy cruiser was having difficulty maintaining station near the *Houston*, and visibility was so poor that the *Boston*'s bridge had to rely on telephoned reports from the fantail to maintain her distance. Things would be easier once the rig was complete and some space could be opened between the two ships.

Finally Miller abandoned the search and substituted a tight-line lashing for the missing pin. It was a calculated risk—the first of many. The lashing had only a marginal chance of holding, but the pin might never turn up. If the two parted at the shackle, the *Houston* would have to recover at least 45 fathoms of anchor chain—by hand, again—just to be able to start over.

Although it seemed much longer, it took just over an hour to rig the tow. As the *Boston* began to pull away, the *Houston*'s forecastle crew partially released the brake on their ship's capstan to begin slowly veering out her anchor chain. By midnight, with 45 fathoms of chain veered, the tow was proceeding at four knots. Even that slow speed was enough to improve the *Houston*'s stability.

Just before midnight, steering control was returned to the *Houston*'s bridge from emergency steering aft. For the time being this was not much of an improvement, since the rudder was still jammed in a hard right position. The attempts of the men in after steering to muscle the rudder amidships had not succeeded, so it was virtually impossible to line up a tow directly astern of the *Boston*. At best the tow could proceed at an angle of 45 degrees from dead astern, which meant that the *Boston* would be working twice as hard as was required by straight-line tow conditions. The tow was deplorably inefficient. More significantly to those on the scene, however, it also meant that the slow-moving ships would take twice as long to get beyond the range of land-based Japanese torpedo planes.

Beyond that, Miller had doubts about the length of the anchor chain that had been veered for the tow. A chain is supposed to sag beneath the surface of the water, dampening the towing cable and reducing the chance of parting the rig. If it is too short it will snap free of the water, twanging like a great bowstring and terrifying all within sight or hearing. Before long the *Houston*'s anchor chain began doing this. Miller and Steuckert were so concerned about the weak towing shackle that they mounted a night-long vigil on the forecastle. It soon became obvious that 45 fathoms of chain did not provide enough catenary to dampen the heaving of the two cruisers. The following morning Miller's deck force veered another 45 fathoms of anchor chain.

The members of this impromptu deck gang, drawn mostly from the second division aft, were learning quickly, working under the worst possible conditions. This enforced on-the-job training would become the rule rather than the exception on board the *Houston*. Since nearly two-thirds of the crew were no longer on board, the remaining men had to perform tasks they would not have dreamed of tackling earlier. This they did—with intensity if not always with relish.

For several hours a great deal of the *Houston* crew's attention had been focused on the immediate problem of rigging the tow. The feverish pace of work below decks had not slackened, however. If anything, it had intensified as the night wore on and more sailors joined damage control parties trying to confine the flooding below the main deck. Bucket brigades were organized, both to bail out compartments and to pass uncontaminated diesel fuel to the men who were trying to put the 60-kilowatt emergency generators back in operation.

At the same time Carpenter Schnable's men began a task that would occupy them continuously for days. There was an unending need to shore up the bulkheads and watertight doors—especially those aft of the engineering spaces—that were beginning to buckle under the relentless pressure of progressive flooding. The *Houston*'s rolling, in combination with the surging action of free-surface water in the partially flooded compartments, had caused several bulkheads to move and their single shoring setups to collapse. Schnable's men attempted to solve the problem by using a tunnel-shoring technique. They ran shoring from the deck to the weakening bulkhead, ran additional shoring to the overhead, and then tied it all together with angle bracing. As daylight of 15 October approached, it appeared that the new setups were holding.

Other damage control teams worked to plug smaller leaks, many of which had been caused by rivets popping out under extreme pressure. Shipfitter Second Class Harold Hurd started below to look for open hatches and other sources of flooding when he encountered a sailor on his way topside from one of the messing compartments. Water was still entering there, the man said, but no one could find the leak.

Hurd went into the compartment. As the ship rolled, water rose from ankle deep to nearly waist high on the starboard side. Hurd sloshed his way into the scullery. On one roll to starboard, with the water low around his feet, Hurd was able to shine his flashlight on the base of an insulated vent duct. Water was seeping through it. He ripped the insulation off the side. Water was coming out of the back of the duct. Pulling the insulation away from the back, he saw a small round hole that he could have plugged with his finger. He found a broom, cut off a piece of the handle, and whittled a plug that would stop the compartment's only leak.

The relentless struggle to contain and reduce the flooded areas continued through the night all over the ship. With ceaseless pressure the sea continuously sought new openings. Undamaged compartments flooded progressively as mounting pressure on the flood boundaries loosened pipes, tubes carrying power cables, and other weak fittings.

Nevertheless, it became evident by daybreak that the unyielding will of the damage control parties was prevailing for the time being. The flooding was under partial control. The starboard list of the ship had decreased to an average of 12 degrees. And the towing rig was still holding.

Most of the crew rested on the weather decks while repair gangs worked below. Unspeakably weary, in wet clothes covered with grease and oil, the band of hollow-eyed, unshaven men had fought off the terrors of the night and the pressures of the sea. They had halted, at least temporarily, the momentum of disaster. The *Houston* had survived the night.

After twelve hours of fighting for survival, the crew experienced the first surge of hope and confidence.

CHAPTER SIX

Streamlined Bait

On board the fleet flagship *New Jersey*, the decision to take the *Houston* under tow had kept Halsey's staff busy through the night. The first order of business was to calculate whether the repositioning of carriers to protect the crippled *Houston* and *Canberra* would hamper the air strikes that had been scheduled for the Philippines on 16 October. The staff determined that the most important strikes—on Leyte, Cebu, and Negros—could proceed as planned.

After 12 October, when the Japanese had first been able to mount a reaction to the strikes on Okinawa and Formosa, their propaganda campaign reached new intensity. Japanese claims escalated until their aircraft were credited with the destruction of sixty percent of America's effective naval strength. According to Radio Tokyo, at least twenty-six-thousand American seamen and more than half a million tons of shipping had been sent to the bottom, and the Third Fleet was no longer an organized striking force.

As Halsey's staff labored through the night of 14–15 October, in fact, their opposite numbers in Imperial General Headquarters were drafting the next day's announcement that a total of fifty-three American ships had been sunk or damaged, sixteen of which were reportedly aircraft carriers.[1]

The reasons behind this outburst of outlandish propaganda, officially endorsed at the highest levels, were not immediately clear. Some have since cited a pathology of fear triggered by the long-dreaded penetration of the American Third and Seventh Fleets into Japan's essential sea area. Complete denial might have been one way of coping with such a devastating turn in the war. Furthermore, Japanese strategists had long considered the approaching battle for the Philippines as their last chance to catch enemy fleets at the end of their extended lines of communication, before they could menace the home islands directly. The outcome of this battle, then, could only be reported in terms of total success or total failure—and no one was ready to report total failure.

Radio Tokyo, which Halsey's staff monitored continuously, was putting out news flashes every ten minutes. There was snake dancing in the streets of Tokyo as hysterical citizens rejoiced over their miraculous reprieve from the destructive power of the American fleet. The welter of misguided enthusiasm was beginning to pique Halsey's curiosity. He decided to troll some bait to see if the Japanese really believed what they were saying.

Task Unit 30.3.1, under Rear Admiral Laurance DuBose, had already been formed to escort the *Canberra* and would soon be joined by the *Houston*. DuBose's unit was becoming widely known in Japanese reports as the "crippled remnants of the Third Fleet." Among friends the task unit was known as the "Cripple Division" or "CripDiv 1." Its healthy members included the heavy cruiser *Boston*, light cruisers *Santa Fe* and *Birmingham*, and destroyers *Caperton, Ingersoll, Cogswell, The Sullivans, Stephen Potter, Boyd, Cowell,* and *Grayson.* It took only a slight shift of emphasis to turn the CripDiv into a "Bait-Div" and test the strength of the Japanese hallucination.

To provide close cover for the BaitDiv, Halsey formed Task Unit 30.3.2 under Rear Admiral C. Turner Joy. This unit was comprised of the heavy cruiser *Wichita*, light cruiser *Mobile*, light carriers *Cabot* and *Cowpens*, and five destroyers.

Halsey next stationed Sherman's Task Group 38.3 between

the BaitDiv and the Japanese home islands and withdrew two other carrier task groups eastward, beyond the estimated range of Japanese search aircraft. The trap was now baited and ready to spring, if Japanese surface forces came out to finish off the remnants they visualized as crippled.

Admiral DuBose began to receive encouraging messages from Halsey describing the potential glories associated with his mission and making occasional attempts to allay his misgivings. Halsey's instincts soon proved to be on the mark.

Whether or not he was totally taken in by the exaggerated battle reports of his field commanders, Admiral Toyoda probably concluded that land-based aircraft had sufficiently damaged the American fleet to give the Imperial Japanese Navy something close to an even chance in a surface action near home waters. Around midnight of 14–15 October Vice Admiral Shima's No. 2 Divisionary Attack Force, consisting of two heavy cruisers, one light cruiser, and four destroyers, sortied from the major base at Sasebo, on the Inland Sea. His mission was to find a remnant of the American force and center his attack on its weak points. He expected to find quite a few damaged vessels.

Connected to the outside world only by a towing cable and a blinking light, the crew of the *Houston* was unaware of the forces that had been set in motion. At the time that was probably a good thing, for they had other concerns, the most immediate being a linkup with DuBose's task group. Hopes rose early on 15 October, when the *Houston*'s lookouts sighted the *Wichita* at 0815, shortly after the destroyers had discontinued their search for men in the water. The tedious, lonely tow would continue for nearly three more hours, however, before the rest of CripDiv 1 was sighted and the *Houston* was able to fall in with the formation, steaming in a southeasterly direction. Although the towing speed still averaged about four knots, the screening cruisers and destroyers had to zigzag at twelve knots or better to minimize their vulnerability to submarine attack.

At the time the *Wichita* was spotted, she was on her way to join Admiral Joy's task unit, operating in support with the carriers *Cabot* and *Cowpens* fifteen to twenty miles away. Knowledge that air cover was nearby provided some comfort to the men of the BaitDiv. They would have been much more comforted, however, by the knowledge that Halsey had deployed his task groups in a way that had left them under the potential cover of more than half the carrier-based aviation available to the Third Fleet.

As things stood then, the men of the *Houston* were aware of these facts only: that their towing speed was miserably slow; that Japanese bombers were less than an hour away whenever they chose to launch from their nearest land bases; that their destination, Ulithi, was still 1,200 miles away; and that the nearest land was nearly 4 miles straight down. The demands of remaining afloat did not leave the crew of the *Houston* any time to ponder their tactical predicament.

Exhausted damage control teams continued to brave the darkness, the fetid air, and the surging water below decks while nonstop shoring, plugging, and pumping continued. They were making some headway. Bucket brigades had succeeded in removing water from the four spaces on the second deck, which had sustained some flooding. That left the second deck essentially dry for the first time since the torpedoing.

Despite the initial success of the submersible pumps, however, fourteen spaces on the third deck were still flooded, either partially or totally. Below that, the four main machinery spaces were still completely flooded, and there was no real hope of dewatering them with the equipment on hand. Forward of the no. 1 fireroom, three magazines were flooded completely and eight others were partially flooded.

As for structural damage, the main longitudinals around frame 81 were seriously buckled. This damage had been caused by the whipping motion and subsequent sagging of the hull. Both the second deck and the main deck had serious bulges in the vicinity of frame 74, where the low-pressure turbine had been driven upward by the force of the torpedo's explosion.

Finally, the no. 1 main engine was demolished, its shaft parted at the reduction gear. The displacement of the shaft ruptured bulkheads 79 and 91 and the no. 1 steam line.

Wind and sea conditions were improving, and the list to starboard continued to decrease as partially flooded compartments were dewatered, but the ship was still in a precarious condition. She was drawing 34 feet forward and 30 feet, 4 inches aft, giving her a mean draft of 32 feet, 2 inches. Since the *Houston*'s normal mean maximum draft was 25 feet, the increase corresponded to a displacement of 20,300 tons. The *Houston*'s condition 6 (full combat load) displacement was 13,900 tons. This meant that roughly 6,400 tons of floodwater remained on board despite the crew's best attempts to remove it. Their efforts to lighten ship could not be relaxed for a minute, day or night.

The main deck was no longer awash, but the freeboard amidships on the starboard side was only three feet on an even keel. For a number of reasons, a transfer of liquids within the ship was not seriously considered as a means to reduce the list and increase freeboard. First, the wing tanks amidships were inaccessible because of the extensive flooding. Secondly, the submersible pumps—the only means available for transferring the liquids—were all in constant use, pumping out flooded compartments on the second and third decks. Finally, no one could predict the effects of a massive shift of water weight on the weakened hull structure, which was already under heavy strain, or the harm that might be done by still more free-surface water below decks.

Consequently, the crew began to lighten ship by jettisoning topside weight on the starboard side. Major items that went over the side included the damaged Kingfisher seaplane; the starboard catapult; the starboard motor whaleboat; two 36-inch searchlights; smoke generators; about twenty-five tons of ordnance equipment; and armored doors from the upper levels on the starboard side.

More than one hundred twenty tons of gear was jettisoned

This view of the *Houston*'s after section on 15 October 1944, the day following the first torpedo hit, shows her list to starboard. The starboard catapult has already been jettisoned and will soon be followed by the damaged OS2U scout seaplane. The plane's bent wing touches a crane on the hangar hatch cover, which will be blown off by the second torpedo explosion a day later.

in this initial effort. In addition, seven compartments on the third deck were being dried out on 15 October. This combination of factors reduced the ship's total displacement to 19,200 tons—a savings of 1,700 tons. At the same time the list to starboard had been reduced from 12 to 8 degrees.

Not much of the water that remained on board was fresh. The torpedo hit had put the *Houston*'s system for distilling and storing fresh water totally out of commission. The evaporators, just above the point of the hit, had been wiped out, and the regular freshwater tanks were both flooded and inaccessible.

At first, drinking water had come from the gravity tanks at three battle-dressing stations, but this supply soon ran out. The *Houston* still had several wing tanks in void compartments that had been filled with fresh water for ballast months earlier. The water had the distinct bouquet and taste of oil, rust, and paint—but it was potable for anyone thirsty enough.

The ship set up a system for rationing the cooking and drinking water. Since power was not available to operate a flushing pump, the bucket brigade technique provided flushing water for the heads. Flushing water was not needed by those who employed the more primitive technique known as over-the-side.

There was an urgent need for uncontaminated diesel fuel to get the forward 60-kilowatt emergency generator back in commission. The generator would provide power to the anchor windlass and enable the *Houston* to haul in the anchor chain with something more than muscle power the next time she had to rig for towing. By straining the fuel through cloth, the crew was able to remove most of the water and other contaminants—enough, at any rate, to get the generator working on reduced power. For several days that lone generator would be the *Houston*'s sole source of power in the forward part of the ship.

Below the main deck conditions were growing increasingly foul. Without a ventilation system in operation, the air grew thick, damp, and fetid. Mold was already forming. Electrical fires broke out as the humidity permeated electrical junction boxes and switches, creating short circuits.

Added to this danger and the unpleasantness faced by all who had to work below the main deck was the ship's unnerving stillness and the crew's inescapable awareness of the presence of many silent shipmates still trapped in flooded compartments below. Aside from the noise made by repair parties, the only sounds that broke the eerie silence came from the creak-

The haggard faces of the men who survived the *Houston*'s first torpedoing show a variety of feelings on 15 October as a noon chow line is
formed on the main deck aft of 6-inch turret no. 4. The severe list to
starboard still precludes optimism, but some of the men are clearly in
good spirits after fighting off the terrors of the preceding night.

ing of twisted steel and flooded ventilator trunks, and the crashing of free-surface water against the bulkheads in partially
flooded compartments.

All hands were eating and sleeping on the main deck and
levels above. The sick bay had been set up in a cabin on the
main deck. Obviously personal comfort had something to do
with the move topside, but every man was also aware that his
ship was still in an extremely delicate condition and could sink
almost without warning at any time. Every time a man went
below he knew that it might be for the last time.

The *Houston*'s crew continued to improve their situation
the first day after the torpedoing. They rigged a sound-powered
telephone system from the bridge to the forecastle and the four
damage control stations. They also established a sound-
powered link with the after steering room, which was now
being supplied with power from the after 250-kilowatt
emergency generator. With this power restored, the cruiser was
finally able to place her rudder amidships, easing the towing
problem for the *Boston*.

At 1530 the men of the *Houston* assembled on the main
deck aft to say farewell to some of their shipmates who had
failed to survive the previous night. A plank had been rigged on
the starboard side, adjacent to one of the gun tubs. The remains of Fireman First Class James R. Cox and Watertender
First Class Robert M. Cranford, encased in mattress covers and
weighted with 5-inch projectiles, were brought to the scene in
basket stretchers from sick bay.

In the solemn moments that followed the commitment of
their shipmates to the deep, the crew could not help but wonder how many were still trapped in the flooded compartments
below. Most estimates ranged between thirty and fifty. As the
voyage across the Pacific continued, awareness of this mournful cargo would grow in the collective consciousness of the crew
until it provided a constant and pervasive reminder of their
own mortality and of the knife-edge of danger on which they
were living. Even those occasional moments of elation brought

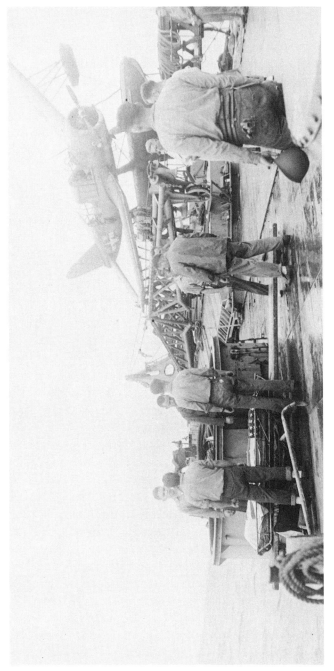

On the main deck aft Captain William W. Behrens (*over left shoulder of man in foreground*) conducts services for a burial at sea on the afternoon of 15 October. Two members of the *Houston*'s crew died the evening before from injuries sustained during their attempt to escape from the rapidly flooding after fireroom.

about by temporary triumphs over the enemy, the elements, and the sea were tempered by memories of silent shipmates.

By nightfall of 15 October the *Houston* was roughly two hundred miles from Formosa, trailing an oil slick nearly fifty miles long. Spirits on board continued to improve despite the agonizingly slow pace of the tow. Each passing hour brought the ship a few miles closer to the point where the threat of air attack would cease to exist. The fact that no attack had developed during the day even fed some hopeful speculation that the Japanese had given up this battle.

On Formosa, however, Vice Admiral Fukudome was still very much in the fight, operating under Toyoda's order of the previous day to annihilate the remnants of the Third Fleet that were assumed to be retiring in defeat. Fukudome harbored no illusions that the battle damage suffered by the Americans was anywhere close to the order of magnitude claimed by the Tokyo propaganda campaign. His private estimate of an inflation factor of three was far too conservative, however. Events would soon prove that his own calculations were overoptimistic by a factor of ten or more.

One consequence of this misreading of American strength was another bad day for Fukudome's aviators. On 15 October, when Davison's Task Group 38.4 struck the airfields around Manila, between fifty and sixty interceptors were either shot down or driven off by the Americans. Fukudome countered with a mid-morning attack that cost still more fighters and light bombers. It succeeded only in inflicting light damage on the aircraft carrier *Franklin*, which sustained a single bomb hit at the corner of an elevator that had been raised to flight-deck level.

By mid-afternoon a second strike group of Japanese army and navy aircraft was launched from Clark Field, on Luzon. Accompanying this ninety-plane group was Rear Admiral Masabumi Arima, piloting a Judy bomber. Arima's dedication was unique at this stage of the war. He had primed himself from the outset of his mission for an effort to make his Judy the first human-piloted bomb in the history of aviation. Indeed, Arima's failure to return to base later that afternoon ignited a stirring tale within Japanese circles: the dedicated admiral, it was said, had crashed into an American carrier and lighted the torch for scores of kamikaze pilots to follow.

The truth proved to be less glorious. Arima's Judy was one of about twenty aircraft that were pounced upon and shot down by Davison's combat air patrol in a battle so one-sided that the rest of the Japanese pilots lost heart and returned to base. None of the planes had come close enough to the ships to launch an attack.

Even as the disparity between Japanese claims and performance grew, Fukudome tried desperately to knock out the BaitDiv. He launched three strikes against DuBose's task unit on 15 October.

The first group of Japanese aircraft ran low on fuel and had to turn back before they could reach their targets. The second group, launched from Okinawa instead of the home islands, was intercepted and punished heavily by aircraft from McCain's Task Group 38.1, screening to the north of the BaitDiv. Fukudome sent a third group out from Formosa in the afternoon. This attack was so timed that, had it been pressed to completion, it could have made a shambles of the *Houston's* burial-at-sea ceremony, but the flight commander's aircraft developed engine trouble and the group turned back.

Meanwhile, Shima's No. 2 Diversionary Attack Group, led by the heavy cruisers *Nachi* and *Ashigara*, continued to close in on Halsey's "streamlined bait"—the BaitDiv's second nickname for itself—with cautious yet deliberate speed, steaming past Okinawa in a southeasterly direction.

CHAPTER SEVEN

"We'll Stand by You"

For the crew of the *Houston*, unaware of Fukudome's determined attempts to shatter their lives, the night of 15–16 October passed uneventfully, in welcome contrast to the one before.

Damage control and repair efforts, along with the jettisoning of topside weight, continued around the clock. Men coming off duty with their working parties sought sleep wherever and whenever they could find it. One small contingent found the time and energy to gather on the signal bridge shortly after dusk for an impromptu song fest, a temporary escape from the reality that enveloped them. In some small ways life was returning to normal, or seemed to be.

Shortly before dawn the next day reality struck again. Two electrical fires broke out simultaneously, harbingers of trouble that would continue to plague the *Houston* throughout her journey.

Electrician's Mate Third Class Alex Macaw was manning the after emergency steering control panel in a compartment just below the aircraft hangar when a fire erupted with an explosion that threw nuts, bolts, and rivets throughout the compartment. Flames shot up all around the switchboard.

Macaw had spent a good part of the previous day collecting bottles of compressed carbon dioxide for fire-fighting purposes, so he had a good supply of it with which to react immediately. The fire, however, could not be brought under control, and he almost succumbed to the smoke that filled the compartment. Fifteen minutes after the fire began, a damage control party with emergency breathing equipment arrived to haul the semiconscious Macaw free of the compartment and extinguish the flames.

The sixteenth of October was not off to a good start.[1]

At daybreak the fleet tug *Pawnee* and an escorting destroyer joined the formation. The *Pawnee* and her sister ship *Munsee* had been ordered to join Task Group 30.8, the fleet oiler group, on 8 October. They were standing by at sea and ready to respond rapidly when the call came for their services.

After wind and sea conditions had begun to improve on 15 October, the *Munsee* had picked up the tow of the *Canberra* from the *Wichita*, freeing the cruiser for combatant duties again. The *Boston*, with a flag officer on board, was anxious to pass her own tow to the *Pawnee*.

There were other valid reasons, generally left unspoken, for passing the tow. At four knots the tugs could maintain towing speed nearly as well as the cruisers they relieved; and two cruisers creeping through the water and bound together made a much more lucrative target for Janapese aircraft than one cruiser and one tug similarly disposed.

Miller's forecastle crew now faced the laborious task of recovering 90 fathoms of anchor chain before the *Houston* could make ready to pass the tow to the *Pawnee*. This time they would have help from the anchor windlass, powered by the 60-kilowatt emergency generator they had recently got working. Efforts to decontaminate the fuel had not been totally successful, however, and the generator would have to operate on substantially reduced power.

The chain was recovered very slowly, at a rate of about two links per minute. This stretched the task out to nearly three hours, but even so the partial power was a vast improvement over the manhandling that had been required on the night of 14 October.

Miller was anxious to see his towing shackle. He was amazed that the jury-rigged lashing—the one substituted for the missing retaining pin—had held so well. Something must have been working in the *Houston*'s favor. But what?

Finally the answer came as the towing shackle hove into view. The lashing had not held, after all. The shackle bolt had begun to back out of its hole, but pressure from a link of anchor chain had jammed it into a canted position. In effect, that had locked the shackle tight before the bolt could drop out and break the tow.

Briefly, Miller pondered the advantages of being born lucky. The monkey on his back began to pout.

By 0915 the passing of the tow began. Conditions were not favorable. The early morning fire in Macaw's compartment had knocked out the *Houston*'s emergency steering control panel as well as the distribution board for the auxiliary 250-kilowatt generator located aft. Once again the *Houston* was unable to control her rudder. The weather was improving, but even though wind and seas continued to abate, there were heavy swells, a by-product of typhoons in the region.

As the *Pawnee* made her approach and attempted to lay her port bow along the *Houston*'s starboard side, well forward, a swell pushed her upward and sideward into the larger ship. During the hard collision, the *Houston*'s starboard anchor became fouled on the *Pawnee*'s port bulwark, adjacent to the tug's own 3-inch gun. The screech of heavy metal tearing filled the air. The anchor sheared off, crashing through the bulwark and the tug's main deck.

That portion of the *Pawnee*'s deck was directly above the messing compartment of the tug's chief petty officers. Two of them were drinking coffee in the mess when the anchor came tearing through. They hurried topside, unhurt but not unstartled.

Simultaneously, on board the *Houston*, the bitter end of the parted anchor chain was whipping violently across the forecastle, threatening to slice off the legs of any man not quick enough to hurdle it. Everyone on the scene—including Commanders Miller and Broussard—made the required jump safely.

The collision had shaken the *Pawnee* hard enough to make her main chronometer jump off its regular time by several seconds. There appeared to be no other serious after effect, however, and the hookup proceeded smoothly after the initial jolt. By this time the *Houston* had fashioned a proper retaining pin for her towing shackle, and she veered 60 fathoms of anchor chain. In combination with the *Pawnee*'s towing cable, this was long enough to provide a catenary that dipped 50 feet below the surface of the water.

An hour and a half after the passing of the tow began, it was complete. The *Houston* was riding easily in tow as the *Pawnee* took station about two-thousand yards off the starboard beam of the *Canberra*.

The other crippled cruiser provided the *Houston* with a new link to the outside world. The *Canberra*'s radios were still operating, and she had been maintaining a handle on the developing tactical situation. As the *Pawnee-Houston* combination drew near, she sent a blinker message welcoming them to the "Streamlined Bait Group." This thoroughly mystifying greeting was partially clarified by a look at the horizon. Around the two cripples a screen of cruisers and destroyers rotated clockwise at 15 knots in a standard antiaircraft defense pattern.

Among the *Pawnee*'s muster of 105 officers and crew were some well experienced in salvage and towing work. They searched their memories for instances of other "twin-towaways." As it turned out, there had been none in either the U.S. Navy or foreign navies.

As the formation plowed ahead doggedly, the *Pawnee*—with the more difficult towing task—became the unofficial guide ship. The tug made slight course changes to compensate for the *Houston*'s jammed rudder, and the entire formation followed suit. Significant changes were few, and the base course remained 130 degrees true.

On board the *Houston* things were looking up. The continuous pumping and jettisoning were easing her stability problems. The starboard list had decreased, and the ship's rolling had lessened. She was not taking as much green water over her main deck as before.

The weather also continued to improve. The sky was hidden behind a high cloud ceiling. A 15-knot breeze from the northeast was most welcome in light of the inability of the slow-moving ships to make their own wind-over-deck. The sea was now calm, although the swells persisted. The *Houston* continued to trail an oil slick, which lay on the smooth surface of the water like a shiny highway stretching to the horizon and beyond.

At 1340 the formation was alerted to the approach of Japanese aircraft when puffs of smoke from exploding antiaircraft rounds appeared in ragged patterns above the screening ships directly astern. For the first time since she had been torpedoed, the *Houston* went back to general quarters.

Fukudome's aviators finally found the crippled remnants they had been seeking. A reconnaissance plane had sighted the BaitDiv at 0920 that morning, about the time the *Pawnee* began to tow the *Houston*. The Japanese reaction to the sighting was immediate. A flight of ninety-nine fighters and bombers was launched from Kyushyu, but their mission was abruptly—and mysteriously—canceled en route. The strike was presumably called off by Admiral Toyoda himself, since his orders of 15 October called for his entire fleet to pursue the *Houston* formation. At any rate, another flight of 107 aircraft took off from Formosa at 1000. In a little over three hours they reached the entrance to Luzon Strait, where the streamlined bait was plodding along at four knots.

Before they could swoop down, the Japanese had to contend with Admiral Joy's close screening force. Fighters from the light carriers *Cabot* and *Cowpens* were already in the air, waiting for the attackers. The outnumbered American aviators plunged courageously into the Japanese formation, shooting down an estimated forty-one aircraft in the ensuing melee. Most of the remaining Japanese scattered, never to see their intended targets, but three aircraft managed to penetrate the screen and press the attack home.

Brief reports by flashing light and plumes of smoke from burning aircraft—sighted well over the horizon—gave the crew of the *Houston* a partial picture of the air battle then under way. They continued their own preparations for the attack.

This time conditions would be different. Instead of going to battle stations below the main deck, all hands moved topside. The pumping of one of the flooded 40mm magazines was halted. Wherever it was possible to improve watertight integrity, material-readiness condition AFIRM was set.

This time there would be no antiaircraft protection offered by the 5-inch mounts. Soon after the torpedoing on 14 October, emergency power had been rigged to two 5-inch and three 40mm mounts, but it had been wiped out by the electrical fire on the morning of 16 October. The 5-inch mounts could not be operated at all and the 40mm mounts had to be operated manually.

Despite this drawback, all 40mm and 20mm mounts were manned. The gun crews, who communicated with the gunnery and air defense officers to coordinate and direct their fire, were makeshift—drawn from roughly one-third of the original crew—but they wanted to make the most of this challenge. Their first real targets were less than ten minutes away.

At 1348 a twin-engine Frances torpedo plane came into sight, heading directly for the *Houston*'s stern, flying over the oil slick that trailed in the ship's wake. By the time the pilot had closed to about five thousand yards, the screening ships ceased fire to avoid hitting the ships in the center of the screen.

It was now up to the *Houston* to stop the attacker. All of the

The twisted wreckage of a 20mm-gun mount is mute evidence of the second torpedo's force. Moments before the hit, the 20mm gunners on the starboard side had been firing into the sea in an unsuccessful attempt to detonate the streaking torpedo before it reached the ship.

The USS *Houston* under attack, as seen from the destroyer *Stephen Potter*.

cruiser's 40mm guns that could bear on the target erupted on command, riddling the aircraft and tearing a large hole in its left wing. The plane wobbled, but the pilot continued his relentless approach.

At a range of about three thousand yards and an altitude of about seventy-five feet, the pilot launched his torpedo. Rather than break off his attack, he continued flying directly into the *Houston*'s murderous automatic weapons fire, an unusual action that can be explained only by the theory that dropping the torpedo was his last conscious act. As the battered aircraft flashed by the cruiser's starboard side at eye level with the signal bridge, Signalman Rooney saw the aviator slumped over his instrument panel, probably dead.[2]

The Frances, riddled by fire from both the *Houston* and the *Pawnee*, passed within two hundred yards of the *Houston*'s starboard side, crossed the forecastle at masthead height, and crashed into the sea without burning, about three thousand yards dead ahead.

The long and narrow torpedo shot from directly astern of the *Houston* left little margin for error. The 20mm gunners shifted their fire from the Frances and concentrated on the fleeting shadow of death that raced through the water toward them.[3] They had to destroy the torpedo before it destroyed them. The rest of the crew could only stand by helplessly, witnessing their own destruction from ringside seats.

In a spectacular explosion the torpedo struck the starboard side all the way aft, near frame 145 and the aviation gas storage tanks. Again the force of the explosion was directed upward, but this time the *Houston* was luckier. Directly above the point of impact was an empty airplane hangar. It had a large hatch at the level of the main deck through which a Kingfisher seaplane could be lowered. A crane used for moving aircraft was resting on the hatch cover at the time of the hit.

A small amount of the force was absorbed by the ship, a large amount dissipated into the empty hangar space. The hatch cover, made of light metal, rose high on a column of fire and smoke and sliced the crane neatly in two. The hatch cover itself remained intact for a surprisingly long time before it disintegrated, spraying the weather decks with shrapnel.[4]

Two 20mm-gun mounts, on the fantail, were located near the point of impact. All but one of the ten men who kept these guns in action were blown over the side of the ship by the explosion.

The volunteer gunner in one of these mounts, recently promoted Chief Watertender Clarence Miller, directed a steady rate of fire at the attacking aircraft before he and part of his gun tub were blown into the air and plunged into the sea.[5] Miller was never seen again. The only man in the area who was not blown over the side, Chief Turret Captain John Greenlee, had been stopped short when the blast slammed him into the port catapult. Badly injured, Greenlee was dragged to safety by Gunner's Mate First Class William Stevens, who had fought his way through a furious gasoline fire to reach the injured man's side.[6]

When the attack started, Electrician's Mate Second Class Campanella had been in the after steering compartment, just below the fantail. A young sailor—the one Campanella had stopped from jumping two days earlier—yelled a warning to him through an open escape hatch. Campanella scrambled up the escape tube leading to the main deck. As he neared the top the massive explosion lifted him through the open hatch and into the air. Floating helplessly for a moment, he saw a mushroom of debris and shrapnel flying upward, carrying Chief Miller and his gun with it. Campanella landed on the main deck, near the no. 4 6-inch-gun turret. When he regained control of his legs, he crawled under the turret. Thoroughly shaken, he vowed to himself that he was not going to press his luck by staying on board for a third torpedoing.[7]

Nearby, just forward of turret no. 4, Electrician's Mate Third Class Macaw was standing next to Seaman Second Class Gymal Cline. Seconds after the explosion Cline fell dead at Macaw's feet, killed by flying shrapnel.[8] Some of the sailors on the main deck, seeing him fall, thought that the weather decks were being strafed by Japanese aircraft. They redoubled their efforts to find any available cover.

The explosion ruptured the aviation gasoline tanks built into the after hangar bulkhead. This touched off a spectacular fire that engulfed the fantail and quickly spread to the trailing oil slick, endangering those men in the water who had been blown over the side and others who had jumped to avoid the flames sweeping across the fantail. They now struggled desperately to keep from being swept into the inferno that blazed on the surface of the water. Some would not survive.

The air attack had not yet ended. Minutes after the torpedo hit, screening ships began firing at another Japanese aircraft approaching from astern. The plane crashed into the sea, slightly abaft the *Houston*'s starboard beam.

Suddenly a Kate torpedo plane appeared on the *Houston*'s starboard quarter, heading fast and low for the light cruiser *Santa Fe*. The *Houston*'s remaining automatic weapons began firing and scoring hits. At a range of about two thousand yards the plane released its torpedo. The *Santa Fe* made a sharp turn in time to avoid the torpedo, which passed astern and exploded harmlessly at the end of its run.

The pilot of the Kate had been frustrated, but he was not finished. He continued to bore in toward his target, taking heavy punishment from the *Santa Fe*'s gunners. In its final moment the plane burst into a fireball and, from a distance, appeared to crash into the cruiser's forecastle. Those who had a closer view saw the aircraft fall into the sea just off the *Santa Fe*'s starboard bow. The ship sailed through a spectacular ring of flames that wiped out one of her forward gun crews.

In the *Santa Fe*'s sick bay, Machinist's Mate Les Quay was recovering from burns and a broken ankle following his rescue from the sea two days earlier. He had listened helplessly to the sounds of battle above decks and watched with concern as the burn victims of the final Japanese attack were brought below. To his shock and dismay, Quay recognized a shipmate from the

Houston, Private First Class Lewis Cardozo, who—after being rescued himself on the night of 14 October—had volunteered to man a 20mm-gun mount again. Cardozo, burned horribly, did not live long.[9]

Throughout the air raid, the *Pawnee* kept her fate firmly linked to that of the *Houston*. The tow line never went slack; she continued to pull the burning cruiser on a steady course at a steady speed. The situation posed several risks for the fleet tug, the most obvious one created by her inability to break free and maneuver for her own safety under air attack. A less obvious but inherently more dangerous risk lay in the fate of the *Houston* herself.

The cruiser had been in danger for two days. Any number of things less traumatic than a torpedo hit might have caused her to break up and sink rapidly once her weakened keel finally gave way. If the *Houston* had gone down with her anchor chain still shackled to the towing cable, the *Pawnee*'s towing winch and other deck gear would have been stripped loose; the strain might well have been enough to "trip the ship," tilting the tug sharply enough to make her capsize. To prevent this, the *Pawnee* stationed a leading seaman in the stern of the tug. In an emergency his task was to light his acetylene torch and quickly burn through the steel towing cable.

Even after the *Houston* was torpedoed a second time, the skipper of the *Pawnee*, Lieutenant James Lees, was determined not to break the tow if he could possibly avoid it. He wanted Captain Behrens to know this. But he also wanted to know whether Behrens had anything else in mind, such as abandoning ship.

Lees called for Signalman "Papoose" Evans and dictated a short message to him that was sent to the *Houston* by flashing light moments later: WE'LL STAND BY YOU. There was no reply, so Lees assumed that his statement of intent had been agreeable to the *Houston*.

The brief message was more than agreeable. It gave the strongest assurance that any man in combat can give another—that he will risk death rather than abandon his brother-in-arms. For the crew of the *Houston*, the message from the *Pawnee* could not have come at a better time.

The growing self-confidence they had nourished through their steadfast and heroic actions of the two previous days had been shattered again in an instant. Many of the men had gone against their own better judgment and fought down the urge to abandon ship after the first hit. Now, after the hammer blow of the second torpedo hit, their world was suddenly an inferno. They felt doomed, and they looked it.

The *Pawnee*'s reassuring message was a help. But the *Houston* was still in deep trouble.

CHAPTER EIGHT

Turning Point

While debris was still raining down from the massive explosion, Commander Miller ordered a damage control party to rig a pair of 2.5-inch hoses from the forecastle. They would use the 60-kilowatt generator to power an emergency fire pump located in the extreme bow, four decks down.

To minimize the danger of the canvas hose being cut by shrapnel during an attack, Miller had forbidden his fire fighters to lay it out in advance. When the hangar fire started their response was rapid, and they quickly led the hoses down the port and starboard main deck, aft to the raging flames.

Ensign Robert Rock had been stationed near the emergency fire pump, but when the damage control party moved forward to activate the pump he was nowhere in sight. The main-deck hatch leading down to the fire pump space was sitting open, mute evidence of Rock's fate. Evidently he had been on his way up when the torpedo struck, and the violent vertical oscillation of the ship's bow had popped him out of the hatch and over the side. Rock was recovered by a screening destroyer, *The Sullivans*, and delivered back to the *Houston* a day later.

The cruiser's starboard gasoline tank had contained about

twenty-five hundred gallons of aviation gas, which had been blown upward into the hangar and outward through the new hole in the stern, where it fed the blaze that had started on top of the oily water. To make things worse, the exploding torpedo had blown the contents of a rag stowage compartment throughout the hangar and the rest of the fantail. The gasoline-soaked rags added to the furious fire.

Faced with this spectacular inferno, the crew began to fire back, slowly at first. Some set about rigging gasoline-driven handy billy pumps, which could put out 50 gallons of water per minute. Others, looking for a way to help, began throwing carbon dioxide bottles into the fire. This had no visible effect on the blaze, burning furiously by then, but it triggered a mood of defiance within the crew. They were emerging from the shock of the violent explosion. Once again they stirred themselves into action. Soon foam was pouring into the hangar from three duplex proportioner hoses fed by the handy billy pumps. Within minutes the fire fighters were regaining control and the aviation gas was beginning to burn itself out.

A stubborn blaze still persisted in the after compartments below the main deck. It could not be reached by water and foam sprayed from topside. Someone had to take the lead, so Miller donned a rescue breathing apparatus, grabbed one of the 2.5-inch hoses, and dragged it below. When he climbed back to the main deck a few minutes later, all the major fires were out.

Barely twenty minutes had elapsed since the torpedo hit, but word was coming down from the bridge for all hands to abandon ship. Miller could not believe it. He raced for the bridge, where the captain, the executive officer, and the department heads had assembled. He argued his case furiously, if not eloquently, claiming that the fire was out. There had been some more flooding aft, but the key bulkheads just forward of the hangar appeared to be holding. The ship was not sinking; she was under a steady tow, in formation, and they still had a fighting chance to bring her back. This time Captain Behrens agreed more readily and rescinded the order.

The effect of the second torpedo hit on 16 October can be seen in this photo of the *Houston*'s stern section, taken en route to Ulithi. Even though the sea is relatively calm and the ship's list has been reduced, the flooding of all spaces aft of bulkhead 136—in combination with the earlier flooding amidships—has left the cruiser riding dangerously low in the water.

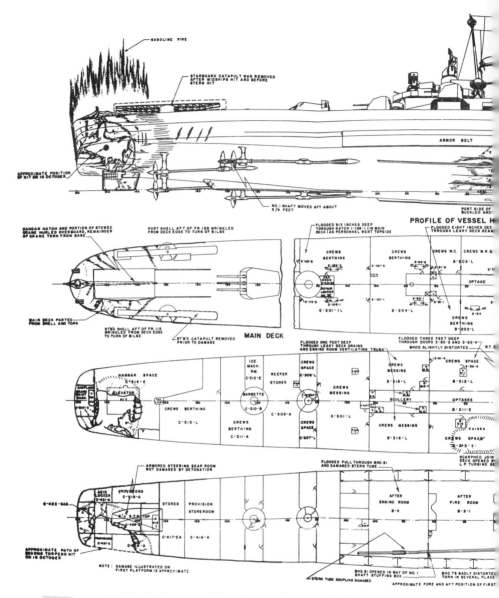

A Bureau of Ships' diagram of the *Houston*'s torpedo damage.

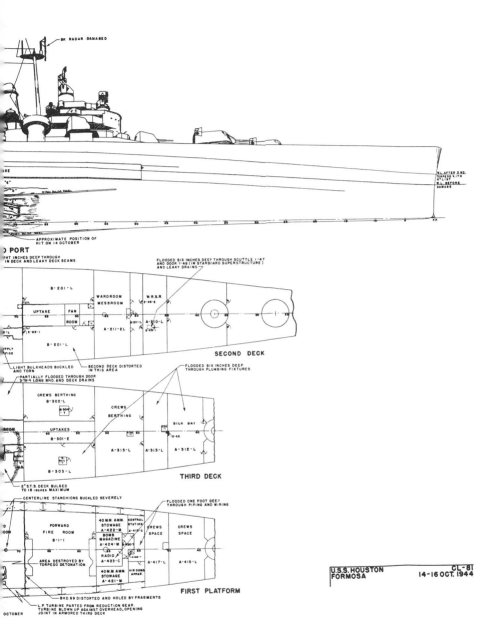

SK RADAR DAMAGED

W.L. AFTER END.
TORPEDO WITH
6° LIST
W.L. BEFORE
DAMAGE

F.P.

APPROXIMATE POSITION OF
HIT ON 14 OCTOBER

D PORT

HT INCHES DEEP THROUGH
IN DECK AND LEAKY DECK SEAMS

FLOODED SIX INCHES DEEP THROUGH SCUTTLE 1-47
AND DOOR 1-48 (IN STARBOARD SUPERSTRUCTURE)
AND LEAKY DRAINS

B-201-L

UPTAKE   FAN
          ROOM

B-201-L

WARDROOM
MESSROOM

A-211-2L

W.R.S.R.

A-210-L

SUPPLY
FICE

LIGHT BULKHEADS BUCKLED
AND TORN

SECOND DECK DISTORTED
IN THIS AREA

PARTIALLY FLOODED THROUGH DOOR
3-78-4 LONG. BHD. AND DECK DRAINS

SECOND DECK

CREWS BERTHING
B-302-L

UPTAKES
B-301-E

B-303-L

CREWS
BERTHING

A-315-L   A-313-L

FLOODED SIX INCHES DEEP
THROUGH PLUMBING FIXTURES

SICK BAY

A-312-L

THIRD DECK

2" S.T.S. DECK BULGED
TO 18 INCHES MAXIMUM

CENTERLINE STANCHIONS BUCKLED SEVERELY

FLOODED ONE FOOT DEEP
THROUGH PIPING AND WIRING

FORWARD
FIRE ROOM
B-1-1

AREA DESTROYED BY
TORPEDO DETONATION

40 M.M. AMM.
STOWAGE
A-422-M

BOMB
MAGAZINE
A-424-M

RADIO
A-423-C

40 M.M. AMM.
STOWAGE
A-421-M

CENTRAL
STATION

CREWS
SPACE

A-417-L

AIR COND.
APPAR.

CREWS
SPACE

A-415-L

FIRST PLATFORM

BHD. 69 DISTORTED AND HOLED BY FRAGMENTS

L.P. TURBINE PARTED FROM REDUCTION GEAR.
TURBINE BLOWN UP AGAINST OVERHEAD, OPENING
JOINT IN ARMORED THIRD DECK

OCTOBER

U.S.S. HOUSTON   CL-81
FORMOSA   14-16 OCT. 1944

Soon afterwards the *Santa Fe* moved close aboard. Admiral DuBose called over with a loud hailer, asking if the *Houston's* situation was hopeless. Behrens' reply came quickly: "Not hopeless, grave."[1]

Grave it was, but as damage control reports and estimates arrived on the *Houston's* bridge, it became increasingly clear that the ship was not in immediate danger of sinking.

Like the first, the second torpedo hit had been accompanied by violent low-frequency vibrations of the hull, which intensified the buckling of the longitudinal strength beams. A vertical crack had developed in the no. 5 port main-deck longitudinal, and the no. 3 and 4 starboard main-deck longitudinals had buckled amidships. When the ship rolled, the after part of the hull actually wagged slowly, like a dog's tail. The explosion had also shaken a number of vertical shores out of position on the second deck amidships. Plating was wrinkled the full length of the main and second decks.

In the after portion of the ship, all spaces aft of bulkhead 136 were flooded, most of them totally. The hangar and the elevator pit lay open to the sea, and the free-surface water in the hangar boomed with every roll of the ship. The steering gear room beneath the hangar, from which Campanella had made his spectacular exit, was almost undamaged, but a few rivets in the overhead had popped, and the space was flooded to a depth of four feet.

Damage control teams suspected that a number of void spaces in the hold forward of bulkhead 136 were flooded as well. Only one of these, however—between frames 126 and 132—was later found to be full. At the time it was impossible to sound any of the other voids to check for flooding.

On the third deck, farther forward, the water in three previously flooded spaces—the ones that had been partially opened to the flooded machinery spaces below them—had risen another foot.

One of the more serious consequences of the second torpedo hit was the partial flooding of the after emergency diesel generator room in the hold abaft the after engine room. Water had entered this space through the no. 2 shaft stuffing gland in bulkhead 101. As the water approached a depth of two feet it ground out the generator. The no. 2 shaft alley flooded completely when water entered through the stern tube.

If the torpedo had struck farther forward, the flooding probably would have been far more extensive, even fatal. At the moment, however, the *Houston* was drawing 31 feet, 6 inches forward and 32 feet, 6 inches aft. Her mean draft of 32 feet was actually 2 inches less than it had been on the morning of 15 October after the first hit. This apparently anomaly could be attributed to the flat shape of the stern and the significant change of trim brought about by the new flooding, which re-

Even in relatively calm seas, the rolling of the *Houston* causes the free-surface water in her flooded and partially flooded compartments to surge violently and relentlessly. In this picture the water in the damaged hangar pounds against the ship's bulkheads, which threaten to give way.

Extensive shoring, installed by Carpenter Les Schnable and his "lumbermen," supports the hangar bulkhead at frame 136. The constant pounding of free-surface water in the damaged hangar placed severe stress on this section of the bulkhead. A similar forest of four-by-fours on the third deck amidships quickly acquired the nickname Schnable's Woods.

duced the ship's list to starboard from eight degrees to six degrees.

The drafts after the second hit corresponded with a displacement of roughly 20,300 tons. This represented an increase of 1,100 tons of water on board, which largely offset the buoyancy that had been gained by the pumping and jettisoning carried out for two days.

In addition to decreasing the starboard list by twenty-five percent, the loss of buoyancy aft changed the *Houston*'s overall trim; she was no longer down by the head but had a trim by the stern. This relieved some of the strain and sagging that the ship suffered when both her forward and after sections were relatively buoyant and the burden of floodwater was being carried amidships.

On balance, the cruiser's stability was decreased by the second torpedo hit. Furthermore, the ship's rolling and the pounding of the free-surface water in the damaged hangar aggravated the *Houston's* condition. For the moment the only encouraging news was that the bulkhead just forward of the hangar was holding, and that damage control parties were already on the scene feverishly installing the shoring that would reinforce the critical bulkhead and confine the major flooding to the hangar area.

It became clear that the crippled cruiser could not support a crew of 550 men without adequate electrical power, ventilation, drinking water, cooking and sanitation facilities, or living facilities below the main deck. After some discussion Captain Behrens agreed with Miller's recommendation to transfer to other ships all but officers, chief petty officers, and any volunteers whose shipfitting and communications skills would prove useful to the rescue of the ship. Behrens signaled the task group commander and requested assistance in taking off three hundred members of the *Houston's* crew.

On board the task group flagship *Santa Fe* word was passed to gun crews to halt their preparations to sink the *Houston*, since her total abandonment was no longer planned. At 1535 the transfer began. High seas and the *Houston's* heavy rolling meant that no other ships could be brought alongside. Three destroyers fell in astern of the cruiser, still being towed by the *Pawnee* at four knots. As the destoyers *Ingersoll, The Sullivans*, and *Stephen Potter* each approached in turn, an increment of one hundred men would be ordered over the *Houston's* starboard side for recovery by the trailing ship.

During the transfer process Miller became a hawk-eyed talent scout, closely inspecting each increment of departing men, prepared to persuade anyone of potential value to the upcoming salvage effort to remain on board. However, Miller would take only true volunteers, no matter how skilled an individual

A close-up of the shoring on the forward side of the hangar bulkhead at frame 136 shows a cylindrical fueling boom being used as a vertical support for the overhead and a side cleaner's stage running horizontally across the bulkhead.

of lesser motivation might be. No one yet knew the extent of the demands that would be placed on those who stayed on board the *Houston*. But their commitment had to be total. Fortunately the pool of potential volunteers was greater than the means available to support them.

Electrician's Mate Alex Macaw donned a life jacket and joined the first group of men ordered over the side. As he stepped over the lifelines he expected a fall of at least twenty feet into the water, but because of the lack of freeboard on the starboard side, he entered the water without a splash. Coffee beans floated all around him. The blast had opened a stores compartment. The beans made Macaw imagine that hundreds of frightened rabbits were floating in the area. A deep drowziness overtook him—it had been a long, traumatic day, beginning with the early-morning fire and explosion in the after emergency steering space and his subsequent rescue from that smoke-filled compartment. Now, with the combination of fatigue, warm water, and sudden relief from tension, he dozed off as he floated away from the *Houston*, held upright by his life jacket.

Eventually Macaw was awakened by rifle fire. Bullets were hitting the water around him. He thought he had come face to face with a Japanese destroyer, then recognized the approaching ship as a U.S. Navy destroyer. My God, they must have decided we are Japs! he thought. When Macaw and the rest of the first increment were recovered by the *Ingersoll*, the riflemen on

A sailor from the *Houston* is pulled on board the destroyer *Stephen Potter*, 16 October 1944.

board the destroyer said they had seen sharks and were trying to frighten them away. Macaw had not considered that possibility while he was in the water, and was just as glad that he hadn't. The thought of sharks might have spoiled his nap.[2]

At that time Vice Admiral Shima's Second Diversionary Strike Force was a good 350 miles from the scene. And he was increasing his distance from the Americans. On the morning of 16 October Shima had been refueling his screening ships from the heavy cruisers *Nachi* and *Ashigara*, east of Okinawa, when he was attacked by two aircraft from the carrier *Bunker Hill*. Shima was able to fight off the attack, but he began to wonder about the allegedly diminished striking power of the so-called remnants of Task Force 38.[3] Within a half hour Shima had decided to reverse course and move away from the Americans. His suspicions were confirmed by a message that afternoon. It was from Fukudome, who advised him that more than six carriers were still operating east of Formosa.[4] Fukudome's searching aircraft had discovered two intact carrier task groups.

However pleased with his decision Shima might have been, he did not fully appreciate how close he had come to falling into Halsey's trap. At 1435—less than an hour after the land-based air attack on the BaitDiv—American search aircraft had spotted Shima's strike force over three hundred miles away. Because of communications problems, however, the report of the sighting was delayed a full hour before it reached Mitscher and Halsey. By then it was too late to launch a strike against Shima.

The carrier *Independence* launched night attack aircraft later that evening, but the Japanese force escaped further detection until it was picked up by American submarines on patrol around Formosa—out of Halsey's reach—days later. By the scant margin of a single hour Shima had been spared. He would play a final anticlimactic role in the upcoming Battle of Surigao Strait.[5]

Even though Shima's surface forces had escaped almost certain annihilation, the combination of Halsey's BaitDiv ploy and Japanese willingness to believe their own propaganda had produced devastating results. In five days of operations near Formosa the ships and planes of Task Force 38 had engaged nearly one thousand Japanese aircraft. More than four hundred of those had been encountered near or en route to the American task groups at sea. The heavy Japanese counterattacks on the carrier groups had been conducted exclusively by land-based aircraft, which had been the nemesis of the Asiatic Fleet years before and which were still considered by some experts to be the certain victors in any duel with ships at sea.

Halsey proved these experts wrong. In the process of fighting off the Japanese counterattacks, Task Force 38 destroyed 807 aircraft, sank twenty-six ships, and reduced the extensive air facilities that could have assisted in the defense of the Philippines. And he did this without losing a single American ship. The freshly demonstrated ability of the fast carrier forces to protect themselves while carrying out devastating strike operations was taken as a healthy sign by American planners, who were then preparing for operations closer to the Japanese home islands.[6]

Despite his dramatic success, Halsey did not emerge unscathed. During this same five-day period seventy-six U.S. Navy aircraft were lost in combat and thirteen others were lost through operational failures. Sixty-four pilots and crewmen did not return from their missions.[7] These losses were not taken lightly, but Japanese air losses were so catastrophic they marked a distinct milestone in the war.

The Japanese themselves later commented that this particular week divided the naval air war into two periods. During the first period they possessed adequate numbers of land-based aircraft, instructors, pilots, mechanics, and fuel. During the second period severe shortages appeared in each of these categories. Even the production standards of the Japanese fell noticeably as they worked in desperation to make up for their losses.

During their series of strikes at the American carrier forces, evidence appeared that the Japanese were having difficulty mounting coordinated attacks. After the strikes coordinated attacks were impossible. Adequate supplies of personnel and materiel no longer existed. The Japanese were being driven to resort to the kamikaze, the only aspect of the war in the Pacific that had not been anticipated years before by American strategists.

By mid-October 1944 an understanding of the extent and significance of their heavy air losses had not penetrated the highest councils in Japan. The drumbeat of propaganda continued and the victory hysteria in Tokyo intensified. On 16 October Tokyo Rose proclaimed once again the sinking of the *Houston*, and an official communique described the sinking of eleven American carriers, two battleships, three cruisers, and one destroyer or light cruiser. In addition it claimed that eight carriers, two battleships, four cruisers, one destroyer or light cruiser, and thirteen more unidentified ships had been damaged; at least a dozen more had been set afire.[8]

With their fears about the outcome of the war dispelled for the moment, the people of Tokyo were ecstatic. Mass celebrations of the "glorious victory of Taiwan" were again held throughout Japan. The Japanese headquarters in the Philippines even joined in, assuming that the long-feared American invasion had been stopped in its tracks, once and for all vindicating Japanese strategy.

Halsey decided to set the record straight. He sent a message to Nimitz, who subsequently released the following to the waiting American public: ADMIRAL NIMITZ HAS RECEIVED FROM ADMIRAL HALSEY THE COMFORTING ASSURANCE THAT HE IS NOW RETIRING TOWARD THE ENEMY FOLLOWING THE SALVAGE OF ALL THE THIRD FLEET SHIPS RECENTLY REPORTED SUNK BY RADIO TOKYO.[9]

CHAPTER NINE

Organizing for Survival

The members of BaitDiv were unaware of their passage through such a significant point in the war. For the moment they were totally occupied in the center of their screen with the task at hand—recovering three hundred men from the *Houston* while ships on the outer rim stood guard.

Despite swells too heavy to permit the use of small boats, the transfer was completed smoothly in about an hour. On board the *Houston* preparations began immediately for a more somber job, and at 1646 a second burial-at-sea ceremony was conducted. This time the crew rendered final honors to Seaman Second Gymal Cline, killed on deck in that day's air attack, and Chief Machinist's Mate Ralph Kistler, who had finally succumbed to burns received after the first torpedoing.

Barely two hundred men remained on board the *Houston*, and six of these were too badly injured to transfer to another ship until small boats could be used again.

Miller wasted no time assembling his salvage group, which consisted of twenty officers and seventy-five enlisted men. He reminded them that the battle for survival was far from over, and that no matter how badly things might go the salvage group would not abandon ship. They were the only hope of saving the ship. They had already destroyed two perfectly good Japanese torpedoes, and they had to be ready to do more of the same.

Miller, who still had a searing recollection of his difficulties rounding up an experienced deck crew to rig for tow, decided to spread out the talent, dividing his men into three salvage parties. That way another torpedo hit or similar misfortune would take out one party at most and leave two duplicates to continue their efforts to save the *Houston*. Lieutenants Steuckert, York, and Simpson would head the parties that worked in the forward, midships, and after portions of the ship, respectively.

As a former destroyer sailor, Miller was accustomed to situations in which there were never adequate resources to go around. He was adept at setting priorities. The biggest shortfall he faced in the damaged *Houston* was a lack of electrical power. The sole power sources consisted of a 60-kilowatt emergency generator and a few inadequate portable gasoline-driven handy billies for pumping water. The survival of the ship might ride on the power allocations he made among the competing requirements for pumping, welding, lighting, ventilation, and cooking, among others.

Miller announced the initial set of guidelines. The cooks would be able to fire up their electric ranges for three hours a day—one hour each for breakfast, dinner, and supper. During the remaining daylight hours the priority would go to pumping compartments free of floodwater, the action that would have the most positive effect on the ship's stability. During hours of darkness welding projects would take priority—especially fastening stiffeners to the buckled longitudinal beams amidships. To minimize the power devoted to artificial lighting, topside projects had priority by day and below-decks projects had priority by night. Ventilation was a problem impossible to tackle. The crew would have to continue living topside while mold and corrosion burgeoned below the main deck.

All the men who had not been assigned to the three salvage

parties were organized into sanitation and messing details. They remained on call to assist the salvage parties. Less than one out of five original crew members remained on board, a fact that required a round-the-clock effort for all hands. A larger number, however, would have overtaxed the ships's ability to support the crew.

At 1820 on 16 October the *Houston* darkened ship and waited for whatever the night would bring. The threat of Japanese air attack persisted, but another more immediate problem arose. Darkness approached, and the weather and sea were making up again.

The *Houston* rolled more and more violently, until the starboard side of the main deck was submerged in green water on every roll. The crew could hear the groaning of metal against metal as the damaged longitudinals amidships suffered further punishment. The seas that surged through the torn hangar severely strained the bulkhead separating the hangar from the rest of the ship forward. Despite all the shoring that had been put in place that afternoon, water seeped through two doors that had begun to buckle in bulkhead 136.

Concern grew over the ship's ability to survive the night. Miller presented a multifaceted course of action to Captain Behrens, who quickly concurred in his approach to the situation. The most pressing task was a continuation of the one that had taken priority since the first torpedo hit—confining the flooding wherever possible and eliminating as much of the pounding free-surface water as possible to reduce the likelihood of further flooding. This called for the dewatering of relatively undamaged compartments that had been subjected to seepage.

The first space to be dewatered would be the partially flooded after steering engine room. In addition to eliminating free-surface water, Miller hoped that this would enable the *Houston* to recover some use of her rudder, which had been jammed ever since the fire and the power outage early that morning. Rivet holes, through which water had seeped, would have to be plugged before the space could be pumped dry. Once the compartment had been dewatered, a hand hydraulic pump could be used to align the rudder along the center of the ship. This would ease the strain on the tow line and result in greater towing speed—if it worked.

The next candidate for dewatering would be the large storeroom on the fourth deck aft, compartment C-417-EA. The same sequence—first eliminating leaks, then pumping— would be followed. A forward space would be next, the partially flooded damage control central station, compartment A-418-C. Miller next planned to dewater magazine A-421-M, on the starboard side. Magazine A-422-M on the port side would remain flooded, however, to help reduce the starboard list.

The dewatering effort would be the continuous backdrop of a concerted effort to strengthen the damaged longitudinals by installing "T" and box girder stiffeners. Stiffening materials and welding equipment would have to be assembled during the night so that cutting and welding could commence at first light on 17 October. The girders would have to be built up in place, using 0.375-inch and 0.5-inch steel plates that had been stowed on board for damage control purposes. Miller's midnight requisitioning forays at the Boston Navy Yard had accumulated an impressive number of these steel plates—far above his basic allowance for damage control materials—but he would still need more. In effect the *Houston* would have to feed upon herself, suffering additional plating to be cut from her superstructure in order to gain extra strengthening amidships. Although this would complement ongoing efforts to reduce topside weight and enhance stability, it had to be carried out with great care to avoid creating new problems for the ship.

Lieutenant Charlie York was to direct the welding effort, which would benefit from another by-product of the midnight forays in Boston. York had obtained a pair of 200-ampere direct-current welding machines heavy enough to get the job done and far superior to the smaller alternating-current models that had originally been issued.

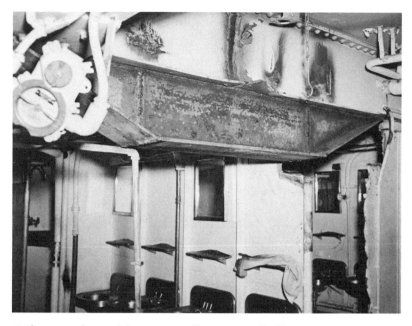

A close-up of one of the many stiffeners installed by Lieutenant Charlie York's welders during the two-week tow to Ulithi. A break in longitudinal no. 5 at frame 81 has been rewelded, and the tapered stiffener (darker metal) has been installed beneath the damaged strength member. Repair work of this type was the most extensive done by any ship's crew at sea during World War II.

Once daylight on 17 October arrived and materials had been assembled, the first attempt at stiffening centered on the no. 5 and 6 main-deck longitudinals on the port side. As the stiffeners were put in place a problem developed. The working of the ship's hull against itself and the further distortion of the longitudinals that resulted brought about a number of weld failures that had to be reworked before anything else could be done. It took two days of steady work to install a box girder on top of the no. 6 longitudinal, an initial triumph that was heartening but did not keep Miller from being realistic. The effect of the girder was similar to that of a wooden splint strapped to a broken or cracked steel rod: There might be some improvement, but the original strength of the rod could not possibly be restored by the splint. It was better than nothing, but would it be good enough?

The question took on increasing significance as the ocean swells grew, an ominous sign that a typhoon was approaching. The *Houston*, with her keel apparently cracked, was riding over the large rounded swells like a limp rag. She still had a severe stability problem as well, appearing to hang motionless at the deepest point of each roll, then shuddering as though gathering strength before her struggle back to the vertical began. The list to starboard and the period of roll had to be reduced.

In addition to the pumping, which of the efforts to reduce the ship's total displacement was by far the most effective, measures to lower the *Houston*'s center of gravity would also

In a priority stiffening effort, a box girder has been installed on the main deck over the damaged no. 6 longitudinal.

bring marked improvement in her stability. Miller initiated an all-hands effort to move approximately two hundred tons of 6-inch projectiles from the second and third shell decks to the lower handling rooms of their respective turrets. At first he had considered jettisoning these projectiles, but he rejected the notion in favor of lowering weight within the ship. A number of the temporary ammo handlers—especially the more senior officers and petty officers—plunged into the task with more verve than their bodies, years away from such manual labor, were willing to support. Before long sore backs were the leading complaint in sick bay.

After the ammunition had been shifted, and after all portable equipment topside—everything that could be spared—had been cast into the sea, Miller turned his attention to heavy mounted equipment. Cutting it away was an intricate business, as illustrated by the work of a four-man party headed by Lieutenant Steuckert. Their primary task was to remove the starboard searchlight and its control unit and heave both pieces over the side. Then they had to cut the searchlight platform into chunks small enough to be manhandled. These, in turn, would be thrown overboard.

Steuckert, working aloft on this project, had to climb up one of the smoke stacks to get to the searchlight platform. At one point he glanced down. The rolling ship was carrying him directly over the water, and there was nothing but an uninviting sea beneath his feet. That was enough to cure him of the habit of looking down.

Fighting off a brief wave of dizziness, Steuckert turned to the task at hand. He and his men worked quickly to rig a block-and-tackle from the searchlight casing to a pad-eye on the smoke stack. Next, using a crow bar, he pried the casing and its drive unit loose from the searchlight's azimuth ring. This permitted some freedom of movement and enabled the working party to hoist the light clear of its moorings by heaving downward on the tackle.

But the light was not yet completely free. Its cables and

wires still stretched down to the platform, and the searchlight itself hung grotesquely in the air like a partially severed head. Steuckert swung an axe with all the force and abandon he could possibly muster on the dizzily moving platform, and the wires finally gave way. Next he dropped steadying lines to the sailors waiting on the main deck, so they could swing the searchlight free of the platform's protective railing. Once the light was clear of the platform it was lowered to the main deck, past the gun shields on the boat deck. After they had disconnected the tackle, the men on the main deck heaved the light into the sea without further ceremony. A brief cheer went up from all within sight.[1]

The removal of the searchlight was hardly a momentous event. It had no noticeable effect on the stability of the ship. But the movement of each piece of topside weight had now acquired the utmost importance in this deadly serious business. Bit by bit, these men were saving the *Houston*. There was little else to cheer about.

Cutting and hoisting and lowering, Steuckert and his men removed the rest of the searchlight and its platform. Then they prepared to attack the searchlight on the port side.

Meanwhile Carpenter Les Schnable and his lumbermen were installing shores to reinforce weakened decks and bulkheads. They found it necessary to shore the deck immediately over the point of the second torpedo hit and to reinstall shoring on the second deck amidships, where the original shoring had been jarred loose by that hit. In addition, the forward bulkheads of the hangar space—nos. 129 and 136—had begun to show signs of distortion at the third-deck level from the constant pounding of the seawater in the hangar itself. Although these bulkheads had survived the explosion and they might have held up without shoring, Schnable's men could afford to take no chances.

After they reinforced the vertical bulkheads, the lumbermen, working from below, shored a section of the hangar deck, which was sagging over the port side of compartment C-417-

EA. With this accomplished, they turned to installing and reinforcing the shoring for all doors and trunks that led to the
flooded engineering spaces.

One other continuous task, also a major one, faced the crew
of the *Houston*. Their ship was a fire trap, and they had to reduce the hazard. In the second-deck living compartments oil-
soaked bedding and clothing had lain about the decks since the
first torpedo hit. Ventilation had ceased at that time, and the
atmosphere was warm, extremely humid, and laden with oil
fumes. Casualty power leads, electric pump leads, and portable lighting circuits had to be strung through these spaces,
which increased the danger of electrical fires.

As topside weight was being jettisoned, Miller and his
damage control teams discarded the oil-soaked materials and
scrubbed down the threatened compartments wherever it was
possible. They could only provide a limited amount of ventilation below the main deck, nowhere near enough to permit the
crew to return to their normal living spaces. To reduce the inci-
dence of short circuits, they attached electrical leads and junction boxes to the overheads of the compartments they ran
through. All these measures undoubtedly helped, but they did
not eliminate the frequent outbreak of electrical fires.

Within two days of the second torpedoing, sleeping, eating,
and working had evolved into a familiar though exhausting
routine. There was a rolling blackout in the ship's equipment
each twenty-four hours as limited electrical power was continually shifted from one area of endeavor to another. Miller's
plan was working.

Despite their grim circumstances, the crew began to eat
passably well once the cooks got their ranges working. There
was enough beef on board—and enough undamaged reefer capacity to keep it—to provide the crew with steak, thus preserv-
ing the ship's reputation as a good feeder even under the worst
of circumstances. And beer from a locker that held recreational
supplies was available for those who had trouble drinking the
water from the void tanks, with its aftertaste of oil, rust, and

paint. The choice of beverage was not as unanimous as one might imagine. Lieutenant (j.g.) Les MacMitchell, a clean-living individual who had been training all his life in hopes of becoming a world-class distance runner, preferred the water. Confronted with the choice in the chow line, MacMitchell turned to the man behind him and asked him what beer tasted like. Commander Cook responded with a rapturous description that compared beer to nectar of the gods. MacMitchell took a single sip, then decided against it. Cook got the rest of the bottle to add to his own ration for the evening. The normal limit was one bottle per evening meal.[2]

By the morning of 17 October the sea was calm enough for a boat from the *Pawnee* to come alongside the *Houston* with a gift of four gasoline-driven pumps and uncontaminated fuel. This marked the end of the cruiser's total dependence on her own damage control resources. From this point on additional shoring material would be passed over by high wire, damaged pumps would be traded for working ones, additional welding materials would be supplied, and even the formidable store of emergency breathing devices and their cannisters—which had barely lasted through the critical period following the second torpedo hit—could be replaced to support the work below decks.

Shortly after receiving the first small boat from the *Pawnee*, the *Houston* had half-masted the national ensign. The crew maintained a respectful silence about the decks as the *Santa Fe* conducted a burial service for their shipmate, Private First Class Cardozo.

The reflective interlude was short-lived. At 1251 a fire erupted near the hangar in a compartment where rags soaked with aviation fuel had been stowed. Breaking out all available fire-fighting equipment—including the handy billies and some fog sprayers that had been rigged to provide saltwater showers—damage-control teams brought the blaze under control within ten minutes.

Despite its brief duration, however, the experience was unsettling. Fire at sea is one of the worst nightmares of any ship, and for one in the *Houston's* precarious condition, aggravated by unusable water mains and limited fire-fighting capability, the prospect was nearly unthinkable. Yet the fire was real.

Fire always posed the threat of explosion. As flames near the hangar were being brought under control someone discovered that three of the *Houston's* 5-inch guns had remained loaded since the first torpedo blast, when their mounts lost electrical power. Would they misfire if the crew tried to clear the guns by firing them in a manual setting? That was probably less risky than trying to clear them any other way. The guns fired. The crew breathed more easily.

But causes for new tension accumulated even as old ones were removed. Despite their claims that both the *Houston* and the *Canberra* had been sunk on 16 October, the Japanese shadowed the BaitDiv with snooper aircraft through the following day. At 1600 on 17 October the *Cabot* reported a number of bogeys in the area. Perhaps the Japanese were gathering for another air attack.

The crew of the *Houston* was grim. They prepared to move to battle stations on the weather decks, but none of the Japanese aircraft approached near enough to be sighted, and the anticipated call to general quarters did not materialize.

The threat of another air attack had a devastating effect on the crew's confidence, which had earlier been shattered on the night of 14 October, when the *Houston* had been transformed from a magnificent fighting ship to a near-lifeless hulk in a matter of seconds. After that first torpedoing, optimism and confidence in their ability to cope with the unexpected had been restored slowly and painfully as the men gained the upper hand in their desperate fight for survival. The second hammer blow of 16 October shattered their hopes once again. How many times could they rebound? How many times could lightning strike? Some of the *Houston's* crew had been on the light cruiser *Helena* when she was sunk by a torpedo. Repeated exposure to the searing experience of being torpedoed in enemy waters tended to be destructive rather than instructive, both for groups and individuals. Everyone had a breaking point, and the benefits of accumulated combat experience had to be balanced against the risks of accumulated combat stress.

Some members of the crew, like Machinist's Mate First Class Horace Harrelson, remained towers of strength despite their harrowing experiences. Harrelson had been trapped inside the battleship *Oklahoma* for about two days after she had capsized during the Japanese attack on Pearl Harbor. Subsequently transferred to the *Helena*, he was on hand for her fatal torpedoing. When Captain Behrens heard of this, shortly after the *Houston*'s second torpedo hit, he immediately sent for Harrelson and told him that he was excused from further duty below the main deck. Harrelson respectfully declined the offer. He said that since he had been a coal miner before he joined the navy, he knew something about shoring and would feel better about the safety of the entire ship if he were allowed to continue in that line of work.[3]

The captain acquiesced, fully appreciative of Harrelson's courage. Sailors who went below the main deck to shore, pump, and weld did so with the certain knowledge that they would be trapped below if the ship got into sudden trouble. And that was not a remote possibility. Despite continuous damage control and repair efforts, the *Houston* was never more than minutes away from breaking up and sinking. Indeed, the all-out damage control effort was absolutely necessary just to maintain that margin of minutes. In the face of potential tragedy, the men of the damage control teams mustered the same quiet courage that Harrelson showed to keep going below day after day, with the unrelieved tension mounting and heightened by fires and air alerts that never failed to bring men surging up from the "salt mines" below decks.

For the time being the crew seemed to be living with the situation. In time, however, the stress would quietly take its toll.

CHAPTER TEN

A Most Delicate Condition

When night fell on 17 October Japanese snooper aircraft were still in the area, but the heightened tension of the afternoon's alert had begun to ease somewhat. For the first time since the previous day's torpedoing, Commander Miller allowed himself the luxury of thinking ahead. The organization of the trimmed-down crew and the plan for allocating resources both seemed to be working, so he could take comfort from the notion that the *Houston* was tackling her problem in an orderly fashion. The size of the problem was still immense, though. They were still well over a thousand miles away from the closest friendly harbor, which, at their miserably slow towing speed, could still take close to two weeks to approach. Every hour would be a battle to stay afloat, with no assurance that even the most valiant struggle would be good enough.

Miller thought back to his discussions with Captain Behrens and the damage control teams. He was clearly on record for his opposition to the idea of abandoning ship. If he had known then what he was beginning to understand now, he might not have been so outspoken. If events proved him wrong, he would *really* be wrong. How many of his shipmates might have to suffer or die because they placed their faith in his judgment? The monkey was still on his back, bigger and heavier than ever.

It soon became evident that Admiral Halsey harbored no such pessimistic sentiments. From the vantage point of the fleet commander it appeared that the BaitDiv had completed its mission and nearly worked its way out of danger. At 2225 on 17 October Halsey detached Rear Admiral DuBose in the *Santa Fe* and the ships of a cruiser and destroyer division from the streamlined bait formation. Rear Admiral Wiltsie, in the *Boston*, took command of the ships still left in the towing operation.

None of the Americans knew it for certain at the time, but Halsey's instincts were on the mark. While his staff prepared the orders to dissolve the BaitDiv, a new sense of reality was taking hold of the Japanese. The army section of Imperial General Headquarters in Tokyo, believing the incredible propaganda claims that had accompanied the fighting around Formosa, had assumed all along that the feared American invasion of the Philippines had been stopped in its tracks. In fact, the staff had even begun to revise the basic Japanese defense plan for the region.

Suddenly, on 17 October, planning stopped and the planners tore up their work. The vanguard of the Seventh Fleet's invasion force had been sighted off Suluan, heading for Leyte Gulf.[1] The sighting, viewed in combination with Shima's and Fukudome's earlier lack of success against the crippled remnants of the Third Fleet, led to an unmistakable conclusion: Japan's defensive posture, instead of improving, had actually deteriorated, and things were getting desperate. Further large-scale attacks on the retiring elements of the Third Fleet would be out of the question for the time being.

At sea, Admiral Wiltsie's CripDiv was not yet receiving any indication that it had worked its way free of danger. More bogeys appeared on American radar screens, and the ships' crews were at general quarters again by mid-morning of 18 October. Once again their protective umbrella of carrier-based aircraft halted the intruders before they could close within visual range of the surface formation. One Japanese aircraft was knocked down and the rest were chased away.

By early afternoon a tanker group had arrived alongside to refuel the *Pawnee* and the *Munsee*. At sundown, upon completion of their operation, the tankers broke away and the towing formation changed course from 120 degrees true to 180 degrees true—from a southeasterly course to one that was due south.

The course change further delayed the slow formation, which was trying to move beyond the range of Japanese aircraft, but a major typhoon had been racing from the southwest to the northwest Pacific, and it was more important for the time being to keep the center of the storm as far away as possible.

The *Houston* had been riding over the ocean swells at the fringe of the typhoon for more than a day. The swells grew, and the main deck on her starboard side was almost continually awash, despite the reduction in the cruiser's list. After a brief period of relatively smooth sailing, stability was becoming a problem again.

There was mounting concern about the residual strength of the buckled and twisted longitudinals. With the swells passing under the *Houston*, the independent movement of the bow and stern sections could be clearly seen; the ship was working against herself. No one knew for sure whether the keel was broken, but there was every reason to suspect that it was. If so, the *Houston* would have little chance of surviving a major storm. She had to take evasive action, even if it meant lengthening her distance from safe haven in Ulithi and temporarily decreasing her distance from Japanese air bases on Luzon, the northernmost of the Philippines.

At this point Miller rearranged his damage control priorities to respond to this major concern. Every bit of available electric power was diverted so that stiffening plates for the heavy longitudinal beams could be cut and welded. Earlier, all hands not involved in the stiffening effort had been drafted to move as much ammunition as possible from the upper handling rooms to the lower ones. The stiffening effort had little visible impact, but the ammo-handling endeavor had shown results. The *Houston*'s rolling decreased, and the main deck on the starboard side was drier.

The night of 18–19 October passed uneventfully. For once, even Japanese snooper aircraft failed to appear.

At 0800 the following morning the salvage tug *Current* joined the formation. The tug came alongside the *Houston* and put an officer on board to survey the cruiser's condition. More importantly, the *Current* passed over a pair of high-capacity submersible electric pumps. This brought cheers from the *Houston*'s haggard dewatering crews.

Buoyed by this fresh evidence that someone outside the CripDiv was interested in the *Houston*'s survival, the crew saw still more of a return to normal by early afternoon. As sea swells began to abate, the destroyer *The Sullivans* had come alongside to receive the *Houston*'s injured by motor whaleboat for further transfer to the *Boston*. These men had been living in an impromptu sick bay on the main deck. Most of them wanted to stay on board the *Houston*, but common sense dictated otherwise.

About two hours after sunset on 19 October another fire broke out, this time because an electric casualty power riser terminal on the second deck short-circuited. Responding quickly, fire-fighting teams had the blaze under control within five minutes. They were getting good at their specialty.

At midnight the towing formation changed course to 115 degrees true. After a thirty-hour detour they were heading once more for Ulithi and away from Luzon. The sea swells continued to decrease, and yet another threat to the *Houston* was sidestepped.

On the following morning, 20 October, reinforcements began to arrive from the east. Two more tugs, the *Zuni* and the *Watch Hill*, joined the formation. The *Zuni* dropped a line astern to the *Pawnee* and the two tugs began to tow the *Houston* in tandem. After the *Watch Hill* had performed a similar maneuver in conjunction with the *Munsee* and the *Canberra*, the formation was able to increase its speed to six knots, nearly doubling the original speed of the towing operation. This was welcome news for every ship in the formation, but particularly for the men of the *Houston*, who could not shake the feeling that their ship was staying afloat on borrowed time.

Since the Japanese air threat was now greatly diminished, the light aircraft carriers *Cabot* and *Cowpens* were detached, with their escorts, from the covering task group. Their departure inspired mixed feelings within the CripDiv. Everyone was glad to see the need for their protective air cover disappear, but no one could forget the way the outnumbered fighters from the two carriers had heroically intercepted and scattered the massive Japanese raid four days earlier.

The operational emphasis now shifted to antisubmarine warfare. A hunter-killer group, consisting of the escort carrier *Hoggatt Bay* and a number of destroyer escorts, began to conduct screening maneuvers from ten to twenty miles ahead of the towing formation.

A snappy six-knot speed of advance was too good to last very long. About ten hours into the tandem tow the line between the *Zuni* and the *Pawnee* parted. This left the *Pawnee* in the workhorse role, while the other tug maneuvered to recover the line. When the tandem tow was reestablished something different was tried. After transferring shoring lumber to the *Houston*, the *Current* proceeded ahead, taking the cruiser in tow in tandem with the *Zuni*. The *Pawnee* dropped out.

The *Munsee* had been freed from the tandem tow of the *Canberra* by a similar maneuver, and the two fleet tugs were detached from the towing formation at 1600 on 21 October. As the *Pawnee* left the formation, sailors on the *Houston*'s main deck gave a good-bye salute to a friend who had stood by them when it counted.

The towing formation was thinning out. The destroyers *Stephen Potter* and *The Sullivans* were also detached, carrying with them two hundred members of the *Houston*'s crew.

Meanwhile, the battle continued against the relentless encroachment of the sea. The *Houston* had left the Boston Navy Yard with a small lumberyard of her own, but she had already used up all the shoring material she carried. The need to install and reinforce shoring below her main deck was never ending. The heavy pounding of the free-surface water threatened to cave in the bulkheads of the hangar and of compartments amidships where heavy flooding had been contained.

With lumber arriving from other ships, Carpenter Les Schnable and his men matched the insistent pressure of the sea by reinforcing the considerable shoring already in place. To contain the flooding in the third-deck compartments over the forward engine room, he installed a veritable forest of four-by-fours, which became known to all hands as "Schnable's Woods."

Even though the threat of a typhoon had subsided and the ship's stability had improved, the effort to lower the center of gravity continued without letup. Armored doors and 40mm-gun director platforms became candidates for dismemberment like the searchlights and their platforms before them. Not all of this material was thrown over the side, however. Salvageable pieces of equipment, down to and including radio tubes, were passed to accompanying destroyers.

The next day, Sunday 22 October, was a bright and sunny one, with the seas considerably calmer. A chaplain had not been on board since the first torpedoing, so Lieutenant Jack Adair conducted divine services on the after part of the main deck at 1100. The worship did not seem to suffer from any lack of professional guidance. It was inspired, intense, and emotional. The men who attended were thankful for their own survival, bereaved over the loss of their shipmates, and moved to a renewed sense of dedication to the task of bringing the *Houston* home.

The emotional release provided by the worship service seemed to break the tension that had been building steadily for over a week. The day was becoming the first relatively good one since the first torpedo hit, and the crew's good fortune increased when, immediately after the service, the destroyer *Bell* pulled alongside to deliver twenty gallons of ice cream. Even to those who were on a steady diet of steak and beer, this was a special treat.

Living conditions on board the *Houston* were beginning to stabilize. The cooks could now bake bread, and only a hardcore complainer would gripe about the lack of butter for it. The saltwater shower system provided relief for the crew, especially those who had to work waist deep in the oily water below decks. They found that Drene shampoo produced the best lather. Salt water was not very good for washing clothes, however, and many men did not bother. Instead they threw their oily garments over the side and wore whatever clean clothes they could find about the ship. Some sailors ended up wearing portions of marine uniforms. Others impersonated marines all the way, complete with caps.

In addition to flooding, loss of stability, and fire, steering was still a major problem for the *Houston*. Men had been working on the rudder for a week since the second torpedo hit, but the tugs still could not tow the cruiser directly astern. Laboring mightily, the after steering crew had wrenched the rudder around by hand to a position of 23 degrees right, where the ship seemed to ride in tow the best. They thought that the rudder might have been bent by the second torpedo blast, but they would have to reach port to find out for certain.

In an effort to help things along, Commander E. S. L. Marshall, the gunnery officer, designated himself unofficial sailing master of the *Houston*. On 23 October Marshall—with Steuckert's forward repair party—rigged a sail on the forestay between turret no. 1 and the bow. With the *Houston* riding so low in the sea and still carrying thousands of tons of floodwater, Marshall did not expect any appreciable propulsive effect, and he was not disappointed when none materialized.

With the wind on the port bow, however, the sail did counter the ship's natural tendency to turn to port because of her funny rudder. So something was gained after all.

Several days had passed since the most recent threat of air attack. Indeed, the towing group was out of range of the severely battered Japanese land-based aviation capability, which was by now incapable of even contesting the landings at Leyte with any strength. The only remaining air threat came from occasional sorties from the smaller Japanese-held islands that had been bypassed during the American drive across the Pacific.

Knowledge that the air threat was now severely diminished was another boon for the crew of the *Houston*, but they did not have much time to enjoy the new situation, for shortly after sunset on 23 October a new threat emerged. The destroyer *Burns*, in a forward station on the port side of the screen, reported a sonar contact and promptly attacked it with depth charges. As the *Burns* left her station in the screen and attempted to close in on the contact, the *Houston* tried to improve her watertight integrity in case of another torpedo hit. Captain Behrens ordered material readiness condition AFIRM set but stopped short of sounding general quarters.

An hour passed, and the *Burns* had not regained her contact. On the *Houston* condition AFIRM was modified to allow some watertight hatches and doors to be opened for ease of passage through the ship. For three more hours the *Burns* searched the area to no avail, then returned to her station.

The rest of the night passed without incident, but the crew of the *Houston* had something new to worry about. The thought of their being stalked from beneath the surface of the ocean was almost more unnerving than the idea of being followed and attacked from the air. Aircraft did not have the endurance to hang around and harass the slow-moving formation for hours at a time; submarines most definitely did. The crew also knew that any attacking aircraft would eventually have to come within range of the *Houston*'s guns. With submarines they had no such assurance. They could not even count on seeing the torpedo that might send their ship to the bottom.

Even the substantial gain in speed of advance brought about by the CripDiv's tandem towing no longer seemed to be a great advantage. The *Houston* was crossing the ocean at snail's pace, and this was no more evident than when, early on the morning of 24 October, elements of Task Group 38.1—their former fighting companions—were sighted on a parallel course twenty-one miles to the southwest. Before long the task group was out of sight, having easily outrun the plodding CripDiv, which was still three hundred miles away from Ulithi.

The towing group would soon have more company. At 0730 that same day Destroyer Squadron 12—with the *McCalla*, the *Farenholt*, the *Woodworth*, and their old friend the *Grayson*—reported for escort duty. A half hour later the *Boston* and five destroyers left the formation, giving command to Captain Early of the *Canberra*. The *Canberra* had to be towed, but she was in much better shape than the *Houston*. The heavy cruiser still had one boiler in operation, her communications equipment was intact, and she was able to provide most of her own shipboard energy requirements.

As the CripDiv neared its destination, the weather improved and the sea calmed. But the tension continued to mount. Another sonar contact was made on 25 October by one of the screening destroyers. Yet another contact was made on the following day. Each time, the towing formation made a 45-degree course change to the south to evade the suspected submarine while the destroyers pursued it, and in each case the contact failed to materialize.

By this time, the men of the *Houston* had been pushed past the point of exhaustion. Despite their stoic acceptance of a dismal situation and their overriding desire to save the ship, they were beginning to show the effects of the strain. For the crew, trapped in an open-ended struggle with the sea, the days were beginning to blur. When from time to time their grinding battle was interrupted by air alerts, fires, or sonar contacts, the men of the *Houston* would temporarily forget their apprehensions and doggedly move once again into harm's way. And these buried fears continued to take their toll, silently, relentlessly.

No one was exempt. Commander Miller had an experience during the final part of the endless voyage to Ulithi that would be a harbinger of later trouble. Another electrical fire had broken out in the stores locker, just forward of the devastated hanger area, and while the after repair party began to fight it, Miller went aft to investigate. When he got there, he saw that the spray from the fire-fighting equipment was not reaching the source of the fire. Someone had to lower himself into the burning compartment to get the job done. It was time for a show of true leadership.

Miller donned a rescue breathing mask and carried a hose into the compartment. He was tied on a tether that was held by sailors on the deck above. The smoke was dense, and he had to feel his way carefully back through the compartment, which was filled with cleaning rags, bedding, and a number of supply items. On his way aft Miller noticed that his arms and legs were almost numb. It occurred to him that his breathing device had run its course; his oxygen supply would soon be depleted. Soon he heard the characteristic crackling sound of a short-circuited electrical junction box. He was almost there. He worked his way in closer to the source and finally put out the fire.

On the verge of losing consciousness, Miller mustered enough strength to pull urgently on the tether line. The men on the other end responded in time to haul him to safety. Dr. Ruoff gave him a sedative to counter the sudden onset of a blinding headache.

Miller gave little more thought to the strange feeling he had had in his arms and legs, even though it seemed after all to have had little to do with oxygen deprivation. Miller finally acknowledged to himself that it was because he was wearing down. But so was everyone else, for that matter.

Then, suddenly, the voyage was almost over. The first part,

anyway. At 0454 on 27 October the *Houston* sighted Falalop Island at a distance of seven miles. The *Current* and the *Zuni*
broke away from the rest of the formation, towing the crippled
cruiser toward Ulithi harbor. Within forty-five minutes they
had made the entrance to Mugai Channel. There they stopped
while the *Current* detached herself from the tow, which was
then shortened for the final passage to the northern anchorage
in Ulithi Atoll.

Commander Ralph K. "Jimmy" James, the repair officer of
Service Squadron 10, had traveled from his main base at
Manus—nine hundred miles to the southeast, in the Admiralties—to meet the *Houston* and assess her salvageability.
What he found was a terribly sick ship. The *Houston* was riding
deep in the water with a list to starboard that she had still been
unable to correct. All her submersible pumps were laboring to
lower the water level in the continuously leaking magazines
and other compartments forward of the no. 1 fireroom, but she
still appeared to be settling deeper into the water. James worried that he might lose her at any moment.

The *Houston*'s superstructure was severely mutilated from
the drastic efforts to cut away topside weight. Her haggard
crew showed the strain of the previous two weeks.

Most disconcerting of all, the *Houston* was a floating mau-
soleum. With the gradual decomposition of the bodies trapped
in flooded compartments below the main deck, the atmosphere
had become infused with the stench of death, making things
extremely unpleasant for the men who remained on board, especially those who had to work below decks. The odor permeated every niche of the ship. There was no place to escape it,
and the crew stopped trying. For many the effect of the smell
was overpowering.

To make the *Canberra* and the *Houston* seaworthy enough
to withstand another tow to the dry dock at Manus, Rear Admiral Carney, Halsey's chief of staff, had ordered Commander
James to bring the repair ship *Hector* forward to Ulithi from
Manus. James had already looked at the *Canberra* that morn-

As the *Houston* enters Ulithi on 27 October 1944, she is already in delicate condition and appears to be settling deeper into the water. There is still no certainty that she can be saved from sinking.

ing and was aware of the substantial repair work that would be required to make her seaworthy again. By comparison, the condition of the *Houston* was incredible. Reason said that she should have foundered days before.

James felt an instant respect for the men whose heroic persistence had brought back the crippled cruiser. But would all their efforts be wasted? James was not sure he could keep the ship afloat, even in a relatively sheltered harbor. He thought of towing the *Houston* to the shallowest part, where she would be relatively easy to salvage after sinking.

Finally, with some misgivings, James decided to proceed with his original plan. The *Houston*'s crew had brought her this far; maybe, with some help, they could make it all the way back. He issued his instructions: The *Houston* would be taken through the submarine nets that guarded the entrance to the harbor and lain alongside the *Hector* in berth 25 of the northern anchorage. She would be in 24 fathoms of water there.

The first leg of the long trip back was ending for the *Houston*. Her crew would never forget the date 27 October. It was Navy Day, 1944.

CHAPTER ELEVEN

"Persistence and Guts"

Within minutes of James's decision, tugs from the harbor arrived to assist. By 0815 the procession was organized and moving up the Mugai Channel, with the *Zuni* towing and five tugs surrounding the *Houston*—one on each bow; one on each quarter; and one trailing, carrying a line from the cruiser's battered stern. A half hour later this conglomerate had passed the channel entrance buoys, and by 1117 the *Houston* was moored alongside the *Hector*.

Three ships, recently damaged in fleet action, steamed past the *Houston* as she was towed up the channel. The cruiser *Birmingham* was riddled with holes of all sizes. The destroyer that followed her looked like a plucked chicken. She had no superstructure at all, no mast and no director, both her stacks were crushed, and her bridge was crumpled up as if it were as fragile as a pasteboard box. But still she rendered passing honors as she moved by the *Houston*. Another destroyer followed whose bridge had been severed from her superstructure as cleanly as though a giant butcher's cleaver had done the job. The crew learned later that all three ships had been stationed alongside the aircraft carrier *Princeton* when she blew up after an air attack.[1]

A welcoming committee of sorts was already on hand. Five of the *Houston*'s officers, who had left the ship in the aftermath of the torpedoings, were coming back on board for duty. Included among them was the ship's senior medical officer, who relieved Dr. Fred Ruoff. The latter had remained on board and performed admirably in the aftermath of both torpedoings.

At 1420 the *Houston* began receiving electrical power from the repair ship, ending her sole reliance on partial diesel power and sometimes-contaminated fuel. Next, saltwater lines were run over from the *Hector* to provide fire mains and flushing water both fore and aft. An hour later the *Houston* was given steam, and an hour after that she was supplied with fresh water from the *Hector*. The *Houston* was wallowing in luxury.

Divers from the *Hector* went over the side and inspected the *Houston*'s bottom to determine the extent of damage amidships. Their report was not encouraging. A huge hole extended from frame 74 to frame 82 on the starboard side, running from the keel out to the rolling chock. The vertical keel had been cracked by that first torpedo hit. The horizontal strap—the massive I-beam—had been severely distorted, but it had held, thus providing the basic longitudinal strength to keep the ship from breaking up. The crack in the vertical keel was a dangerous inch or two wide.

The *Houston* sustained additional hull damage on the way in to her berth. One of the tugs pushing on the cruiser's bow was operating with a worn-out fender slung over her own steel bow. Each time the tug tried to ease up to the *Houston*, riding deep in the water, ground swells pushed her up into the plating on the cruiser's hull—high above the armor belt that would normally protect the larger ship from damage.

Each of these minor collisions punched a small triangular hole in the *Houston*'s hull and generated an impromptu chorus of protest from the bridge and the weather decks of the *Houston*. After all they had been through, the men of the *Houston* would not suffer others to inflict new damage on their battered hull with impunity.

By the time the mooring was completed a dozen of the triangular holes dotted an area four feet square. They were more a nuisance than anything else. Shipfitter Harold Hurd cut a piece of steel plate from one of the remaining 20mm-gun splinter shields and quickly patched the damaged area.

The following morning a team of naval constructors came on board, headed by Rear Admiral H. Travis Smith, the maintenance officer of the Pacific Fleet. Accompanying Admiral Smith were his deputy and a representative from Washington who had been sent out by the Bureau of Ships to evaluate the damage.

The strenuous efforts to save the *Houston* had generated a great deal of interest in the navy's higher echelons. This ship was a test case for the policy of salvaging rather than sinking damaged ships. Other ships had suffered more extensive topside damage and been repaired relatively quickly. But none that had been so gravely wounded beneath the waterline as the *Houston* had remained afloat long enough to consider major repairs. If the *Houston* could ever be made ready for sea again, a long-standing U.S. Navy policy was likely to be reexamined.

Someone aside from the participants in the sink-or-save debate was applauding the *Houston*'s unwillingness to go to the bottom, and on more mercenary grounds. One of Lieutenant York's colleagues in Cruiser Division 14 had found that his own belief in the wisdom of damage control and salvage was putting him directly at odds with his contemporaries. When he first heard that the *Houston* had been torpedoed, his loyalty to York as much as anything else prompted him to bet that the stricken ship would survive. He had a great many takers, especially after the second torpedo hit on 16 October, but he did not waver. Instead, he took all bets, and now he was about to collect.

Unfortunately the first conference with Admiral Smith got off to a bad start, which was to set an unhappy precedent for the numerous inspection visits of the next few weeks. The admiral and his party came on board the *Houston* without being forewarned about the overpowering smell of death coming from the compartments below. Instantly, almost involuntarily, they recoiled from the scene and returned to the relatively odorless *Hector* in great distress, holding handkerchiefs to their faces.

After this initial disruption, Admiral Smith and the other conferees determined that two of the four flooded engineering spaces, the after engine room and the forward fireroom, could be dewatered in Ulithi. First, however, it would be necessary to dry out compartment B-313-L, a large berthing space on the third deck. Watertight doors in bulkhead 79, which connected this compartment to the machine shop, and an escape hatch from the after fireroom directly below had been left open by men trying to scramble topside after the first torpedo hit. As a result the compartment was totally flooded.

On 20 October Commander Miller sent divers into the compartment, but the dangerously surging free-surface water kept them from reaching either the doors or the hatch. The space remained full of water for the rest of the tow to Ulithi. On 28 October divers from the *Hector* had more luck in calm water, and the compartment was sealed off. A large 6-inch salvage pump was used, and the space was dewatered without incident—except for the recovery of a body, the first of thirty-three still trapped below. The remains were identified as those of Machinist's Mate Third Class Ralph Thompson.

Before the pumping began a working party skimmed most of the oil from the surface of the water. They soon learned that their effort was not good enough. The remaining oily scum managed to adhere to everything in the compartment as the water level gradually receded. This left the crew with a massive cleanup job. Their lesson did not have to be repeated. From that point on, the crew exercised exceptional care in removing all oil before they started to pump any compartment dry.

Oil removal was just one of several painstaking preludes to pumping. The major sources of leaks had to be found and sealed before dewatering could begin. In some cases spots were sealed while pumping was under way. This was slow and deliberate work. It took ten days to free the first of the major engineering spaces of floodwater.

Despite this slow beginning, spirits on board the *Houston* had lifted. The crew's desperation at fighting an unending battle with the sea was ebbing. They were gaining the upper hand with the *Hector*'s specialized equipment and her crew's skilled assistance. Morale improved along with living conditions. Most of the *Houston*'s men were able to eat and sleep on board the *Hector*, gaining temporary but welcome respite each day from the stench of death that still permeated their ship. Moreover, a sense of well-being was established now that the threat of air attack was remote. The *Houston* was no longer a slow-moving target on the high seas.

Danger had not entirely disappeared, however. On the morning of 29 October two FLASH BLUE air attack alarms were sounded throughout the harbor, twenty minutes apart. The attacks failed to materialize. The bogeys might only have been snooper aircraft trailing Vice Admiral McCain's Task Group 38.1, which was entering Mugai Channel at the time.

McCain's return to Ulithi signaled the end of one of the largest and most significant naval engagements in history, the Battle for Leyte Gulf, to which the strikes on Okinawa and Formosa had been an important prelude. After a fueling rendezvous on 16 October, McCain's group had joined the carrier task groups of Rear Admirals Bogan and Sherman in a search for the Japanese surface force that had been stalking the BaitDiv. Since Admiral Shima had reversed course by that time and was heading for safety near the coast of China, the search proved fruitless. By 18 October the three carrier groups had rejoined Task Group 38.4 to conduct air strikes on Luzon, part of a larger strategic effort to isolate the intended landing site at Leyte.

The landings commenced on schedule, on 20 October, and triggered the long-planned Japanese counterattack that was designed to split away the American Third Fleet from its support of the Seventh Fleet. Ozawa's northern force, containing carriers but few carrier-based aircraft, would be the decoy for Halsey. With Halsey's own carriers thus drawn north, surface forces led by Vice Admirals Nishimura and Kurita could converge on Leyte Gulf via the Surigao and San Bernardino straits, respectively, to attack the vulnerable amphibious ships.

After the American submarines *Darter* and *Dace* made initial contact with Kurita's force on 23 October, sinking two heavy cruisers and damaging a third, Halsey commenced an air search and made contact twenty-four hours later. He immediately ordered three of his task groups to strike Kurita and ordered McCain—en route to Ulithi for rest and replenishment—to reverse course and refuel at sea. McCain's group had sped on its eastward course past the CripDiv less than three hours earlier. Later on 24 October Halsey's search planes spotted Ozawa's force northeast of Luzon. Halsey decided to race north all night to be in position for a decisive engagement the next day. As things turned out there were three major engagements on 25 October, with the only decisive one occurring when Nishimura pushed his way into Surigao Strait and a classic naval ambush fashioned by Rear Admiral Jesse B. Oldendorf. Halsey launched air strikes against Ozawa, sinking one carrier and badly damaging two others, but he had to turn southward in response to the threat posed by Kurita's force before he could get his battleships within range to administer the *coup de grace* to Ozawa. Despite being heavily outgunned, however, American forces were using every advantage they could extract from wind, rain, smoke, and interior position to turn back Kurita's force near Samar. By this time Kurita, thinking his best opportunities to disrupt the landing had passed, chose not to engage Halsey's forces, which were then racing southward. Kurita made good his escape with a severely diminished but still minor fleet-in-being.

Ozawa was not so fortunate. After Halsey's air strikes he had to contend with a cruiser-destroyer group led by Rear Admiral DuBose, which in a most welcome reversal of their Bait-Div role moved ahead of the carrier groups to pick off cripples and stragglers. Ozawa's sacrifice had not enabled Kurita to break up the landing as planned, but it had forced Halsey to chase two major Japanese forces over six hundred miles without fully engaging either. Kurita was thus able to escape annihilation.

The Battle for Leyte Gulf also saw a brief reappearance of the BaitDiv's would-be tormentors, Shima's surface force. It was last seen heading for the Chinese coast on 16 October, just out of Halsey's grasp. Shima was supposed to team with Nishimura for the attack through Surigao Strait, but hearing news of Oldendorf's ambush, Shima once again prudently withdrew.

Overall, the Americans had saved their amphibious shipping and destroyed the Japanese capacity to fight another major fleet engagement, at a cost of one light and two escort carriers, two destroyers, and a destroyer escort.

Back at Ulithi, joy was spreading over the news of the great victory in the Philippines. For the men of the *Houston*, however, the cost of that victory was quickly felt. On the afternoon of 29 October they gathered on the main deck aft to attend a funeral service for their shipmate Ralph Thompson, knowing that this would be the first of many over the next several weeks. After the service Thompson's remains were taken ashore and buried in a cemetery on nearby Asor Island.

The somber mood created by the funeral lifted later that afternoon when 132 shipmates, who had last been seen struggling in the rough waters off Formosa, reported back on board. This was the first large increment of returnees in a steady flow that would swell the size of the *Houston*'s crew to more than five hundred by the time she left Ulithi. The reunion was marred by yet another BLUE ALERT, which turned out to be a false alarm.

Augmented by the returnees and the specialists from the *Hector*, the crew soon fell into a shipyard routine. Beaches, beer, and limited recreational facilities were available to them, but they still had the enormous task of making their ship seaworthy enough to withstand the next leg of their journey. Ahead lay a nine-hundred-mile tow to a floating dry dock at Manus Island, in the Admiralties, and they had a lot to accomplish before getting under way.

In addition to drying out the two major engineering spaces and the large berthing compartment, they had to dewater the machine shop, the evaporator room, and the forward uptake spaces. The longitudinal beams amidships had to be stiffened with more than the Band-Aid patches that had been put on at sea. They had to restore what buoyancy they could by raising the damaged hangar until it could be partially sealed from the sea. And they had to salvage and restore whatever machinery and equipment they could. By the end of the first week in November they had dewatered the machine shop and the forward engine room and had recovered six more bodies.

On 5 November Ulithi received warning of a severe typhoon approaching the atoll. Commander James was convinced that the *Houston* would sink if the typhoon hit. He approached Admiral Carney, Halsey's chief of staff, and suggested that the ship be moved to shallow water, where she would go down only a few feet, simplifying salvage efforts. Carney agreed.

James began preparations to move the *Houston* to the relatively shallow southern anchorage fifteen miles distant. The *Hector* would pull her there while she was still moored alongside. To prevent the two ships from scraping hulls while they were moored side by side, heavily constructed, shallow-draft rectangular floats called camels separated them. Unfortunately the damaged cruiser's deep draft raised her waterline well above the tough armor belt that extended around the vital midships area of the hull at the level of the third deck. The camel, pushed by the *Hector's* movement, was pressing against the tender hull plating and relatively light framing above the armor belt, which could be easily damaged. It would not have been a problem as long as the ships remained stationary and the water calm, but with the ships under way and a typhoon approaching, the situation would be a crisis.

James knew this and moved a forty-man working party from the *Hector* to the *Houston* to help control flooding. He also put on board the *Houston* dozens of welding machines, burning torches, and portable gas-driven pumps; a great deal of steel plate; and all the shoring material he could assemble.[2]

The *Houston* had just finished burying the five men whose remains had been recovered from the machine shop when word came down to prepare to move to the southern anchorage. Within a surprisingly short time the *Hector* weighed anchor and was moving forward, dragging the *Houston* alongside. Two tugs moved in to assist.

As the ships gathered momentum, a damage control team called for Commander Miller to come to the third deck, port side, forward of frame 69. There Miller could see that the *Houston*'s hull was buckling inward above the armor belt and that the relatively light framing was beginning to bend. Horizontal cracks appeared in the shell plating, which was actually split between frames 55 and 57. Miller notified the bridge but got no sympathy. There was no time to rig another type of tow. They had to get to the anchorage before the storm hit.

The ships moved until darkness fell, then stopped and anchored for the evening. They sailed again at daybreak, reaching berth 671 in the southern anchorage by noon. The *Hector* dropped anchor with the *Houston* moored alongside.

Once again, the *Houston* was in severe trouble, in immediate danger of sinking. As the velocity of the wind increased, the two ships surged together violently and the camels continued to batter the *Houston*'s tender hull. The flooding worsened, despite furious efforts to control it. Lieutenant York and his welders risked electrocution in their attempts to seal leaking seams in the hull. Carpenter Schnable and his lumbermen tried to caulk the seams and shore up the weakest sections of the hull, but they found very few places where the inner bulkheads could withstand the pressure of being caught between the camels and the shoring. All available pumps were in operation to keep up with the flooding.

Miller was halfway convinced that Tokyo Rose held a patent on the shallow-draft camel. The monkey on Miller's back was laughing and scratching and jabbering.

By noon the next day, 7 November, winds had risen to gale force. The *Houston* was losing her gallant fight to stay afloat. The center of the storm was nearing Ulithi, and the water in the anchorage was unbelievably rough.

The time had come for the *Houston* and the *Hector* to terminate their cheek-to-jowl position. The *Hector* hove anchor to short stay, with her engines moving her ahead slowly. The *Houston*, meanwhile, dropped her anchor and veered chain while the mooring lines were singled up and electrical cables, fire hoses, and all other life support connections between the two ships were severed. Below the *Houston*'s main deck the flooding took a turn for the worse when power for the operating pumps suddenly dropped to a single 60-kilowatt generator.

By 1530 the *Houston* had veered chain through her starboard hawse pipe to about 75 fathoms. Captain Behrens gave the order to let go all lines and veer chain to 105 fathoms. Simultaneously, the *Hector* weighed her anchor and backed all engines full, attempting to overcome the wind and wave action driving her toward the *Houston*. On the forecastle, Miller watched the *Hector*'s bow swing toward the low-lying *Houston* as the repair ship moved aft, gathering speed.

A few seconds later the *Hector*'s starboard anchor caught the corner of the *Houston*'s no. 2 5-inch-gun mount, which broke loose from its stops and spun violently in a counterclockwise direction with enough force to turn anyone inside into a scrambled egg. Fortunately the mount was unmanned.

Before she broke clear, the *Hector* damaged another gun mount and carried away the after davit of a lifeboat station. But down below, the damage control people were relieved. At least the repair ship wasn't caving in the *Houston*'s hull any more.

The *Houston* was on her own again, and though a furious storm was raging, the bent anchor, obtained from the *Birmingham* on the second day in Ulithi, was holding; the water was shallow, fifteen fathoms or less; and the *Houston*'s stern was less than three hundred yards from an exotic tropical isle known to the Americans as Pig Island.

The *Houston*'s bridge prepared to ride out a major storm at anchor with a total lack of propulsive power. The damage control people below prepared for a long, grim evening with a very sick ship. James stationed two seamen at the *Houston*'s draft marks, one forward and one aft, to give reports every fifteen minutes on the change in draft. The exhausting pace of the past two days had to be picked up still more under the pressure of the moment. Welders, many working underwater for the first time, patched the damaged hull. The pumps worked to the full capacity of the 60-kilowatt generator.

The storm worsened, and the *Houston* settled deeper in the water. The seamen stationed on the bow and stern reported steady increases in draft. The repair parties, their reserves of strength fueled by desperation, maintained a frantic pace.

Sometime after 0300 the first encouraging report about the *Houston*'s draft came in from the lookouts: no change. A second report brought the same news. The repair parties were holding their own, for the time being, at least. Around 0600, at the height of the storm, the first report of a reduction in draft came in. James felt as though he had been granted a reprieve in a tough struggle he still was not sure he could win.[3] Actually, there was good cause for optimism. While the battle against new flooding continued on the port side, repair crews on the starboard side made real progress in their painstaking preparations to dewater some of the larger flooded compartments.

There was a breakthrough in the after engine room. Earlier investigation by divers revealed that a section of shell plating, in way of the stern tube for the no. 1 shaft, had been pulled away from the hull between frames 103 and 105. Once blankets and kapok life jackets had been packed into the stern tube through this opening, the leak was sealed sufficiently for dewatering to begin.

As the water level in the after engine room dropped, bulkhead 91 was shored from the after side and persistent leaks around the pipelines and cables running through the bulkhead were plugged. Other leaks around the no. 1 shaft at bulkhead 91 and the stern tube were sealed off with welded steel boxes. Once the leaks were stopped, the *Houston* was able to rid herself of thousands of tons of floodwater she had been carrying for three weeks. She was finally getting well, and a day or so later, the typhoon moved on.

On 10 November the salvage tug *Current* came alongside to hook up electrical power, fresh water, and salt flushing water.

The next day brought a message from the commander of the Third Fleet to the commanding officer of the *Houston:*

WELL DONE TO ALL YOUR BOYS FOR BRINGING A FINE SHIP OUT OF THE NIPS' FRONT YARD TO LIVE AND FIGHT AGAIN. THE WHOLE FLEET ADMIRES YOUR PERSISTENCE AND GUTS.—HALSEY.

The "Old Man" may once have had his doubts, but there was no doubt now. He believed in them. A great deal of money changed hands as the disbelievers paid off their bets.

CHAPTER TWELVE

Farewell to Pig Island

Three days after the arrival of Halsey's message the *Hector* moved back alongside the *Houston*, replacing the *Current*. Miller noted with great satisfaction that the offending shallow-draft camels had been put out to pasture and replaced by a considerably more appropriate set of fenders constructed from manila line. Without delay, the *Hector* provided the *Houston* with electricity, fresh and salt water, and steam. A rotating system of repair parties that would work in shifts around the clock was established on the *Houston*.

One major engineering space, the forward fireroom, still had to be dewatered in Ulithi. It took five days to prepare the compartment for pumping, for a number of torn places in bulkhead 69 had to be caulked or otherwise sealed. Divers descended into the space to do most of the work. When pumping commenced, on 19 November, the bulkhead was shored from the forward side and the remaining tears were sealed off by welded cofferdams.

Because of the huge hole in the *Houston*'s hull and the severe damage to bulkhead 79, the two remaining engineering spaces—the forward engine room and the after fireroom—were still virtually open to the sea. They would have to be dewatered in dry dock. By this time, however, divers had been able to recover most of the bodies from the flooded compartments. The remains of thirty men had been buried on Asor Island. It was grim, gut-wrenching work, especially for the hospital corpsmen who prepared the bodies for burial. Once the distasteful task was completed, the overpowering smell of death gradually subsided. It would eventually disappear as those still left below decomposed to a skeletal state.

At 0550 on 20 November the destroyer *Case* reported on TBS broadcast that she had rammed and sunk a Japanese midget submarine outside the entrance to Ulithi's Mugai Channel. A sudden alertness to new danger swept through the ships inside the harbor. Five minutes later there was chaos. The fleet oiler *Mississinewa*, anchored near the entrance to the harbor, exploded without warning, erupting into massive flames that turned the predawn sky into the image of high noon. The oiler burned furiously for two and a half hours before she finally sank. A screen of tugs and small craft hurriedly formed to begin patrolling the twenty-six-mile-long harbor. They eventually located and sank two more midget submarines that had somehow managed to slip past the antisubmarine nets at the entrance to Mugai Channel. This new development was particularly unsettling for the men of the *Houston*, who watched the *Mississinewa* burn. As a stationary target, moored close by Mugai Channel—a double target, really, with the *Hector*—the *Houston* represented an equally likely choice for any other unwanted visitors.

Furthermore, a submarine might not even have to pass through the nets to inflict damage. About the same time as the attack at Ulithi, Commander James had been forced to make a hurried return to Manus, the focal point of his Pacific ship repair enterprise. The ammunition ship *Mount Hood* suddenly blew up in Seeadler Harbor, and everyone on board was lost along with several others who had been waiting nearby in smaller boats and barges to receive ammunition.

The *Mount Hood* virtually disintegrated from the force of

the blast. The largest piece of metal recovered was the size of a card table top. The devastation extended to a radius of 1,500 yards around her; lesser damage was done to ships outside that circle. Thirty suffered some type of damage, and James had to juggle repair priorities to get the least-damaged ones back into service first.[1]

Although the exact cause of the explosion could not be determined, it was soon speculated that a Japanese submarine had lain in wait outside the torpedo nets of Seeadler Harbor. When the nets were opened to allow ships to transit, the sub could have launched a torpedo straight down the channel, catching the *Mount Hood* squarely.

Whatever the cause, the incident did not sit particularly well with the crew of the *Houston*. They knew that their next stop was the floating dry dock in Seeadler Harbor. Where could they go to fix their ship in relative peace and quiet? Tension lasted for about a week and culminated in a warning that a one-way submarine or kamikaze attack might take place. The *Houston* manned half of her antiaircraft guns. There was another FLASH BLUE alert, but no attack materialized and the critical period passed without incident.

Meanwhile efforts to decrease the *Houston*'s draft continued to show steady progress. Before he returned to Manus James made Miller a de facto member of his repair staff and left extra men and materials at his disposal.[2] Work continued in shifts, around the clock.

As the *Houston*'s hull rose higher out of the water the level of floodwater in third-deck compartments gradually receded. When it was down to about three feet repair parties sealed off the ruptured portions of the armored deck, which were admitting water from the flooded spaces below. They laid timbers around the edges of the raised plates of the armored deck, shored them into place, and caulked them. After they had caulked the deck drains in the evaporator room as well, dewatering began. When the spaces were pumped dry, timbers were secured with welded steel brackets and the shores were removed, which permitted the welders to construct a steel cofferdam around the edge of the damaged deck plating. The case-hardened armor plate itself could not be welded with the equipment on hand, but the cofferdam was adequate to hold back the water that still tried to enter the compartment from the flooded engineroom directly below.

The ship still had to regain buoyancy in the flooded stern section, which lay open to the sea. The first step for Lieutenant York and his men was to go underwater and tack-weld a steel bulkhead across the hangar deck. This would seal off the forward part of the hangar. The bulkhead, about 0.25 inch thick and 72 inches high, was placed athwartships by sections in the vicinity of frame 138. There it was welded to the deck and braced. Portable pumps were activated to dewater the forward part of the hangar. When this was nearly complete, the repair crew could see that a small river still flowed under the welded bulkhead. They plugged the leak with oakum, which they covered in turn with four-inch strips of steel plate. Next they installed a four-foot-high longitudinal bulkhead along the ship's centerline, connecting the temporary bulkhead to bulkhead 136. Finally, they placed another transverse bulkhead, also four feet high, to extend bulkhead 136 from the centerline to the port side.[3]

This effectively cut the dewatered portion of the hangar into three sections, which brought a number of benefits. The new compartmentalization promised more effective control of any further flooding. In addition, by removing such a great quantity of the ever-dangerous free-surface water from the forward part of the hangar, they eliminated the need to reinforce the hangar's forward bulkhead. The stress on that particular bulkhead had worried Miller ever since the second torpedoing. This particular bit of repair work reduced the danger of flooding in compartments C-416-A and C-417-EA, below and just forward of the hangar.

With the new bulkheads in place and the forward part of the hangar dewatered, storerooms C-419-A and C-421-A, di-

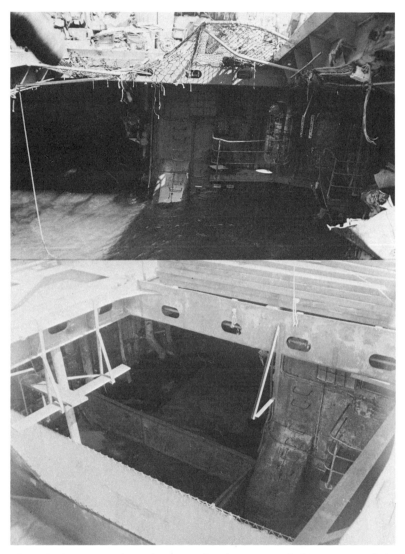

These before and after photographs show partial dewatering of the damaged hangar at Ulithi and temporary bulkheads being installed at frames 138½ and 135 and along the *Houston*'s centerline. The temporary bulkheads will reduce the likelihood of progressive flooding in her stern section during the tow from Ulithi to Manus.

rectly below, could be pumped dry. Again, the repair crew had to work slowly and methodically. Their first task was the decidedly unpleasant one of removing the badly decomposed provisions that filled both storerooms. Divers who entered these compartments through hatches in the hangar deck soon learned that the provisions could be floated out through the same hatches and subsequently removed from the ship through the gigantic torpedo hole at frame 145.

After they had cleared themselves some working space, the repair gang once again sought to seal off leaks in the compartments. In this case, a leaking bulkhead and a nonwatertight door proved to be the culprits. They were quickly sealed and both compartments pumped dry. To permit pumping, the repair gang built wooden cofferdams around the two hatches in the hangar deck that the divers had originally used. After dewatering had been completed, they installed additional hatches in the deck of the hangar to provide easier access to the steering gear room, the storerooms, and other spaces below.

Relieved of the burden of so much floodwater, the *Houston* was riding relatively high, with a draft four to five feet less than she brought to Ulithi. This raised the third deck well above the waterline and enabled the welders and shipfitters to repair the damage that the *Hector* had inflicted on the *Houston's* port side.

One additional hull repair was required to strengthen the stern section for the upcoming nine-hundred-mile tow to dry dock. The large torpedo hole at frame 145 on the starboard side was patched with temporary side plating from the main deck to the waterline. This would provide a partial breakwater against following seas and minimize the free-surface effect in the after part of the hangar.

One other major problem regarding seaworthiness remained. Lieutenant York's welders had fastened a great number of stiffening plates to the twisted longitudinal beams in the ship, but this had offset only a small part of the drastic loss of longitudinal strength. Something more had to be done. Repair gangs set about rigging four groups of "T" beams—on the main, second, and third decks, starboard side, and on the main deck, port side. Each group consisted of three beams, each one 24 inches high with a 0.5-inch web and a 0.75-inch flange. The beams were 176 feet long, and the completed installation would run from frame 57 to frame 101. The three groups of beams on the starboard side were tied together with 6-inch and 8-inch pipe stanchions.

The installation of these massive beams lent an impression of new sturdiness to the *Houston*. But Miller, for one, had his doubts. Even with a great deal of the floodwater removed, the midship section would still be unable to withstand the normal hogging and sagging stresses created by moderate head seas. The *Houston* still had nowhere near her original strength.

As structural repairs progressed, the crew managed to salvage and fix some equipment and machinery. They placed the no. 1 boiler in the forward fireroom back in operation and put an emergency evaporator plant into commission. They got the after 250-kilowatt generator back into service, making it possible to restore the steering machinery and return steering control to the bridge. A forward SG radar went on line, and several battle telephone circuits were reactivated to provide communications between key stations.

The work at Ulithi on the no. 1 boiler set the standard for later work at Manus on boilers no. 2 and 4. It began on 16 November, when the water level in the forward fireroom fell below the upper gratings and the crew was able to enter the compartment.

The repair gang washed down all exposed surfaces with hot salt water and followed that with hot fresh water supplied by the *Hector*. After obtaining a sample from the water gauge drain, they ran a salinity test on the water that remained in the boiler. The sample was salty, as expected, but the boiler could not be dumped at that time because the water in the fireroom was still too deep. Water, backing up through the high-pressure drains on the superheater, kept the boiler full to the air cock. A hose was taken into the boiler uptakes through the inspection door so the repair gang could wash down the inside of the breeching and the exterior surfaces of the economizer tubes with hot fresh water. Then they sprayed the freshly washed surfaces with a rust-preventive compound. At this time they also sprayed external fittings with Consol.

By 19 November the forward fireroom was completely de-watered. The repair crew opened the firesides and removed all boiler air casing doors. Then, using fresh water, they washed out the firesides from the uptakes down to the furnace floor. After that they sprayed the tube banks and boiler fittings with rust preventive.

All the brick work appeared to be intact except for areas that had been soaked by seawater and fuel oil. The chrome ore had softened, and about a third of the studs were exposed on the wall tubes. The outer casings in the rear of the boiler had buckled badly, and they had several small holes. The tube exteriors were in good condition, however, and only one outboard economizer tube was slightly warped.

On 21 November the repair gang was finally able to drain the boiler, after taking care to isolate the high-pressure drains from the flooded forward engine room. They flushed out the boiler and filled it to the air cock with fresh water. Then they applied a hydrostatic test of 420 pounds per square inch. There were leaks only at the superheated handhole plates. By the next day the leaks in the outer casing had been repaired and the boiler dumped. The repair gang opened the watersides, removed the internal fittings, and wire-brushed the steam and mud drums. There was some evidence of corrosion in the steam drum, but no serious pitting had occurred. The tubes were free of scale and pits.

The repair gang flushed out the superheater with hot fresh water on 24 November. They closed the boiler's watersides and began the process of boiling out, using 40 pounds of boiler compound per 1,000 gallons of water. Steam was provided through bottom blow valves and the superheater outlet drain. It took forty-eight hours.

On 26 November the boiler was again washed out carefully. The repair gang replaced internal fittings, closed the water-sides, and once again filled the boiler, this time to a steaming level. Eight pounds of boiler compound were placed inside. The next day they kindled a wood fire to bake the brick work and dry out the insulation. They kept the superheater full of water, with the outlet header valve cracked. They regulated the size of the fire so that a small amount of steam would escape from the air cock drain when any pressure built up.

They put out the fire and let the boiler cool on 28 November. The next day's inspection showed that the brick work was dry. Once again all the tubes were sprayed with rust preventive.

On 2 December a 750-pound hydrostatic-pressure test was conducted with the emergency feed pump operated by high-pressure air. The test was satisfactory. The following day the re-pair gang lighted fires under the saturated side of the boiler, using the smallest size of sprayer plates. In an hour and a half steam pressure was raised to 200 pounds, before the safety valves were lifted by hand and the boiler was secured.

Then came the big test. On 4 December steam pressure was raised to 400 pounds and the boiler was cut in on the auxiliary steam line. Despite the careful preparation, however, the crew still had some doubts about the boiler's ability to withstand high pressure, because the torpedo hit and subsequent flooding had left it in a slightly tilted position. This generated fears about structural weakness.

As the heat built up, the boiler expanded, then developed an ominous bulge. Fireman First Class John Seagraves, who was convinced that it would explode any minute, was able to remain at his station only through a tremendous exercise of will power.[4] But the boiler held.

After five hours of operation, the boiler fires were allowed to die out. The first severe test had given successful results but the gang in the fireroom could never bring themselves to completely trust their boiler.

On 5 December steam pressure was again raised to 400 pounds, and the boiler was given two bottom blows to reduce salinity and water hardness. On 9 December the crew raised the pressure to 500 pounds, setting and testing the safety valves. After a final bottom blow, the boiler was back in commission on 11 December, steaming for auxiliary purposes.

It had taken more than three weeks to get the no. 1 boiler working again. It would be much longer still before that boiler could provide propulsive power to the ship. But at least the *Houston* could now make her own boiler feedwater and provide her own fresh water for drinking, cooking, and bathing.

Days merged into weeks as the repair work continued without letup. On occasion small groups were able to get ashore to Pig Island, which the *Houston*'s crew soon adopted as their own. There, a worn and haggard sailor could relax on the fifty-foot strip of white coral sand that ringed the palm-studded islet. He could swim in the warm, clear waters close inshore. And he could have a can of beer or two.

Soon the end of the stay at Ulithi was upon them. At 0840 on 13 December the *Houston* lit off her boiler and cut it into the auxiliary steam line. The *Hector* disconnected her own steam lines to the cruiser. Later that morning the *Current* came alongside and moored to the *Houston*'s starboard quarter to assist during the final evening of repair work.

At 1600 the last of the big working parties from the *Hector*—three officers and sixty-four enlisted men—debarked. They were relieved by a thirty-man working party that came to the *Houston* to put the final touches on the repair effort.

The next visitor sounded a more ominous note. At dusk a landing craft came along the starboard side and delivered thirteen life rafts. The *Houston*'s crew took this in stride.

As midnight approached, electrical power and freshwater lines to the *Hector* were disconnected. The final thirty-man working party went on duty at midnight and wrapped up its work by 0445.

At 0630 on 14 December the *Houston* once again set her special sea detail and made preparations for getting under way. Eight minutes later the *Hector* was under way from alongside, soon followed by the *Current*. The fleet tug *Arapaho* moored to the *Houston's* starboard quarter to help move her through the channel.

By 0740 the *Houston* was under way. Five minutes later she received a towing cable from the fleet tug *Lipan*. The forecastle crew quickly shackled it to the port anchor chain. Only thirteen minutes elapsed this time before the *Lipan* was able to take a strain on the tow and proceed toward Mugai Channel at a speed of 3.5 knots. Three hours later the *Lipan* and the *Houston* were standing out of Mugai Channel, with the tow wire paid out to 250 fathoms and the anchor chain veered to 60 fathoms.

They made a rendezvous at the channel entrance with the other ships of their towing formation, now designated Task Unit 30.9.14. These were the destroyer escorts *Osmus*, *Raby*, and *Strauss*, and the minesweeper YMS 184. The destroyer escorts quickly formed an antisubmarine screen ahead of the *Houston*, and the YMS 184 took a patrolling station about three thousand yards astern.

The *Arapaho*, with her channel passage tasks complete, moved ahead of the *Lipan* to establish a tandem tow. With both tugs towing the *Houston* the speed of the formation increased to six knots. With her steering restored and her mean draft reduced to 27 feet 6 inches, the cruiser rode easily at the tow.

The formation set a course of 191 degrees true, bound for the Admiralties, where a floating dry dock waited the *Houston's* arrival. By 1700 the southernmost point of Ulithi Atoll faded from the radar screen at a distance of fifty-thousand yards. It was Pig Island, the potential refuge during all of the *Houston*'s troubles in the southern anchorage for anyone who could swim three hundred yards.

At 1723 the formation went to darken ship. As night fell the antisubmarine screen prowled ahead, their sonar systems pinging relentlessly.

CHAPTER THIRTEEN

Dry Dock

Within six hours of leaving Ulithi the destroyer escorts in the antisubmarine screen developed a sonar contact. The *Raby* left the formation at 0145 to track down whatever lurked below.

The men standing the mid watch on board the *Houston* felt the familiar grip of mounting tension once again. A contact so soon! The sub must have been waiting for the *Houston* to come out of the harbor. Despite their recent searing experience they still preferred an occasional threat from the air to a continuous unseen one from below.

Nothing new developed topside during the remaining hours of darkness, but the *Raby* continued her search. At 0700 the formation changed course from 191 degrees to 170 degrees true. Fifty minutes later it abruptly changed again, to 138 degrees.

In mid-morning the *Houston* test-fired all her 40mm and 20mm antiaircraft weapons. The *Raby* reported another possible contact. The formation changed course again, to 228 degrees true. The *Raby* finally lost her sound contact and returned to the formation at 1315.

Below the *Houston*'s main deck Miller and his damage control specialists were grim. They had resumed their war with the sea. And despite their accomplishments, the products of weeks of hard work at Ulithi, they were not getting off to a good start. It was clearer with each passing minute that they still had a severely damaged hull, one that would require constant vigilance.

Welds that had sealed off old leaks were cracking and starting new ones. The extensive hull damage on the port side, sustained in Ulithi, still required close watching by Lieutenant York and his welders and Carpenter Schnable and his shoring gangs.

The greatest focus of concern was the four-foot-high steel cofferdam, which covered the seam that had been opened in the armored deck. Since it sat directly above the flooded forward engine room, this steel box was the key to keeping the third deck from flooding again. In the usually placid waters of Ulithi's lagoon, there had been no problem. At sea, however, all bets were off.

Back near the hangar, another vigil centered on the second major breach in the hull, which was also boxed off by temporary four-foot bulkheads. The ship's battered stern generally rode clear of the sea's surface, with only an occasional dip as the ship rolled to starboard. The hangar situation was considerably less menacing than the problem with the armored deck amidships. Miller still carried a heavy monkey on his back, and all his damage control people were sharing the load.

For the rest of the day the *Houston* conducted general drills. Her crew felt the grip of tension ease as they busied themselves relearning their varied duties at sea. There was little anxiety that evening when, at 2000, the *Strauss* was detached from the formation for new duties elsewhere, weakening the antisubmarine screen.

The next morning a life raft was sighted about two thousand yards from the *Houston* and recovered by one of the screening ships. It had no occupants. Feelings of foreboding returned, particularly to those who had recently clung to rafts hoping for rescue.

They did not have long to dwell on their memories. At 1337

the *Osmus* reported a close-in sound contact at about twenty-five hundred yards. The formation immediately changed course again, while the *Osmus* developed the new contact, which faded within fifteen minutes. The *Osmus* stayed in a search pattern for another hour, unsuccessfully attempting to regain it. The rest of the formation continued to zigzag.

The allotted hour had just ended when the *Houston*'s lookouts sighted something about three thousand yards off her starboard quarter. It looked like a periscope. The *Houston*'s 20mm and 40mm gunners opened fire, hitting the object repeatedly for the next minute or so until it disappeared without a trace. No wreckage. No oil slick. No indication of what had been there.

Radar and sonar contacts abruptly stopped. The towing formation discontinued its radical course changes and once more headed directly for the Admiraltics. They were watchful, and jumpy.

In mid-afternoon the *Houston* made the final contact of the day, on her long-range air-search radar, at forty-eight thousand yards. The unidentified aircraft faded from the radar screen after being tracked for five minutes.

The next day, 17 December, brought a new concern. Up to that point the formation had been receiving sporadic air cover from Catalina flying boats based to the west. These big seaplanes were proficient submarine hunters, but they could provide coverage only out to a range of about four hundred nautical miles from their home bases. As they passed the four-hundred-mile mark, the ships in the towing formation realized that they would be moving through a dangerous gap. It would be twenty-four hours before aircraft based in Manus could reach them, and there were no friendly carrier task forces operating in the area.

It was not hard to draw a parallel with a similar gap in the North Atlantic earlier in the war that placed Murmansk-bound convoys at the mercy of wolf packs of German U-boats during the period that air cover could not be provided. At this time and place, of course, the threat of wolf pack tactics was remote, but even a single submarine that happened to stray across the course of the towing formation could easily make a kill that had eluded hundreds of Japanese aviators.

Despite these misgivings the day passed quickly. The *Houston* made a single long-range surface contact by radar, which was soon identified as an American cargo ship accompanied by a destroyer escort and heading in a northwesterly direction. The next day brought the welcome sight of friendly aircraft overhead—Mariner flying boats from Manus.

Tactically, the worst was over. But below decks the worst was still being realized. The welding and shoring and pumping had to continue around the clock to keep pace with new cracks and leaks that constantly posed the threat of flooding. When the *Houston* crossed the equator, on 19 December—and all hands were mustered at quarters to begin the initiation of polliwogs—the damage control gangs stayed below; they could not be spared even for this traditional seafarers' ritual.

The *Houston*'s radar first picked up land at a range of forty-two miles at 0400 on 20 December. By mid-morning the formation was close enough to Manus Island for a harbor pilot to come on board. The *Arapaho* cast off from the tandem tow and the *Lipan* shortened her towing cable in preparation for entering port. The *Houston* followed suit, heaving her port anchor chain in to two fathoms from the sixty she had veered for most of the tow from Ulithi. Shortly before noon they passed through the main entrance channel leading into Seeadler Harbor and through the antisubmarine net, standing toward berth 222.

An hour and a half later the *Houston* was anchored in fifteen fathoms of water. Relief swept through the crew, especially the damage control gangs. Their ship was still not ready for sea, and they were lucky to have avoided heavy weather on the way to Manus.

Seeadler Harbor looked civilized compared to the barren Ulithi. A great number of American and Australian ships were continually entering and leaving port. Evidence of the *Mount*

Hood disaster lingered, but a feeling of safety in numbers prevailed.

This expansive feeling was short-lived. At 1455 on 20 December—less than ninety minutes after she had dropped anchor—the *Houston* received a FLASH BLUE air attack alert from the beach and promptly went to general quarters. An "all-clear" came a short eleven minutes later. But the *Houston's* crew had been reminded that they were still in the war. Another FLASH BLUE alert came the following afternoon, as if to drive home the point.

The *Houston* was not able to enter the floating dry dock right away. Commander James had to juggle docking priorities on an almost daily basis to meet a constantly changing situation as battle-damaged ships entered the harbor on short notice. Whenever possible, he had the least severely damaged ships repaired first to get them back into action. This policy met with generally unfavorable reactions from the commanding officers. Some, unhappy with their relatively low repair priorities, threatened official acton to get themselves advanced on the waiting list. Others, not anxious to get back on the line, were unhappy with their relatively high repair priorities.

Despite some dashed hopes for extended rest and recreation, the operation at Manus was proving to be one of the true success stories of the war. The more lightly damaged ships were being repaired and turned back toward battle areas in weeks rather than the months that would have been required if they had gone back to Pearl Harbor or points east.

In the case of the *Houston*, though, a fast turnaround was out of the question, even for the miracle workers at Manus. They could hope only to make her seaworthy enough to return to the United States under her own power for overhaul and rebuilding.

The other central member of CripDiv 1, the *Canberra*, was in the floating dry dock when the *Houston* arrived at Manus. Although her internal damage from the torpedo hit amidships did not match the *Houston's*, the size of the hole in her hull was

about the same. To prepare for his own role in patching the
Houston's hull, Lieutenant York went to the dry dock and observed the work being done on the *Canberra's* hull. In the inter-
ests of speed, a team of SeaBees from a Manus-based naval
construction battalion had built a square-cornered steel box to
cover the large penetration hole near the heavy cruiser's keel.
The box stuck out from the hull like a large, square blister,
about thirty inches thick. York didn't think much of this technique and said so in his subsequent report to Captain Behrens.
Even before he became fully aware of the range of talent and
material resources available on Manus, he knew he could do
better.

To install the large temporary patch on the *Houston's* hull
amidships, York planned to build new framing in the torpedo
hole, trimming the outboard edge of each frame to conform to
the curve of the hull, and weld the framing to the new temporary hull plating. The result would be a T-type frame of 0.5-
inch boiler plate welded to a temporary outside hull of 0.25-
inch boiler plate. The old hull plating would be overlapped by
framing on the inside and new plating on the outside.[1] The
Houston might still show a wrinkle or two, but she would be
blister free. York's plan was approved.

On 8 January 1945 the *Houston* entered floating dry dock
ABSD no. 2 in company with the light cruiser *Reno.* It took
about an hour to moor her after she had crossed the sill of the
dry dock with the assistance of tugs. The dock was pumped dry
in only twenty minutes, and the *Houston* was resting on the
keel blocks, high and dry, before noon.

Divers watching the operation closely reported that the
Houston had an extraordinary sag amidships. Someone else
was watching closely. The *Houston* and the *Reno* had scarcely
finished docking when they found themselves to be the center-
piece of that afternoon's broadcast from Tokyo Rose.[2] She announced that the two cruisers had gone into dry dock that
morning and cautioned the American repair gangs not to work
too hard because the Japanese fully intended to sink the ships

along with their floating dry dock. She did not bother to explain how the *Houston* had been resurrected after she had been reported sunk, again, on 16 October.

Some of the men of the *Houston* tried to laugh off the fantastic broadcast; others thought of the air alerts that never seemed to stop. The *Mount Hood* had been blown to bits in this same harbor. The laughter began to sound hollow. It stopped completely at 1420.

Another FLASH BLUE air alert was sounded and the *Houston* went to general quarters. This time she was truly a sitting duck. All that passive air defense plans could dictate was flooding the dock, minimizing damage to it and the ships in it.

The all-clear was sounded and the crew went back to work. They were tired of being yanked in one direction and then another. Each new alert was like sandpaper being rubbed over their raw nerves, reminding them that their battle was not yet over but that a single bomb or torpedo hit could easily bring it to an abrupt end. The closer they got to winning their battle, the more intolerable the thought of attack became.

Now that the *Houston* was clear of the water, the first order of business was dewatering the forward engine room and the after fireroom. These compartments soon yielded the last of the cruiser's mournful cargo, the skeletal remains of the last five missing shipmates. Only one positive identification could be made, on Fireman First William T. Walsh, recovered from the after fireroom. The other remains matched the number of names still on the list of the missing.

After all the remains had been recovered the ship's colors were half-masted for a final funeral service on the main deck aft. One sailor from the *Reno* also received final honors. A burial party then left the ship for the Allied Armed Forces Cemetery on Manus.

When the ship's colors were two-blocked again at the conclusion of this sad duty, the *Houston* entered a new phase of her struggle for survival. Now, with the missing crew members recovered and accounted for, the survivors could move ahead,

A detail from the *Houston* renders final honors as a shipmate is buried at the Allied Armed Forces Cemetery on Manus. The recovery of remains from previously flooded spaces when the *Houston* was in dry dock finally accounted for all the "mournful cargo" the cruiser had carried for nearly three months.

free of a particularly painful debt to the past. Some of the living owed a great deal to the men they had put to rest—most notably, the heroic Machinist Carl Behrend, who had lost his life in the act of saving others.

Once again there was little time to reflect. The *Houston* braced herself for an influx of salvage and repair specialists. Her crew would be augmented by 150 SeaBees from four naval construction battalions, as well as men from a number of nearby tenders and repair ships. Two repair gangs would be formed, one to work amidships and one to fix the damaged stern. The crew themselves would have to match the efforts of the repair gangs from Manus, man-hour for man-hour. Work would continue around the clock.

The influx of all this new talent brought a shift in roles for Miller and his principal damage control assistants, Lieutenants York and Simpson and Carpenter Schnable. Instead of keeping the ship afloat, their prime task would become planning the repair work in coordination with Commander James, then supervising it closely to ensure that the repair gangs that swarmed over the ship were not working at cross-purposes.

Also a matter of major concern was the danger of fire,

In dry dock at Manus, the *Houston* shows extensive wrinkling on the starboard hull plating aft of 6-inch turret no. 4. Directly below, the propellor and no. 1 shaft have been displaced aft by five and a half feet. When the first torpedo explosion broke the coupling of the reduction gear, the propellor drag pulled the shaft out of position, causing a major leak in the after engine room.

With the *Houston* high and dry in the floating dry dock at Manus on 8 January 1945, the extensive hole running from the starboard bilge keel to the centerline keel in the vicinity of frame 75 is visible for the first time.

which had grown considerably. Despite the best efforts by damage control gangs at sea and at Ulithi, the *Houston* had been a firetrap since the first torpedo hit. Now the fire hazard was being compounded by the introduction of cutting and welding torches, by power cables strung throughout the ship, and by the increase in oily rags and other combustible materials. A carelessly dropped cigarette butt could easily ignite a blaze.

Carpenter Schnable was the fire chief, and with Miller's blessing and encouragement he ran a tight, hard-nosed operation. His objective was to reduce the fire hazard while facilitating the work of the visiting specialists. He did not always succeed in the latter, but he had to succeed in the former.

Meanwhile, since work continued around the clock, coordination and supervision were required around the clock. Among themselves, Schnable, York, and Simpson would be able to keep Miller abreast of things, but none of the four would be able to sleep or relax much.

After Miller inspected the *Houston*'s hull beneath the waterline, he was convinced that the ship would not have survived the tow to Ulithi without a lot of luck and some help from above. The hole in the ship's bottom, opening into the forward engine room, measured 32 feet, fore and aft, by 24 feet. The center of impact was in the vicinity of frame 75, roughly 16 feet from bulkhead 79 and 24 feet from bulkhead 69. The bottom side of bulkhead 79 was severely crumpled and split, but the

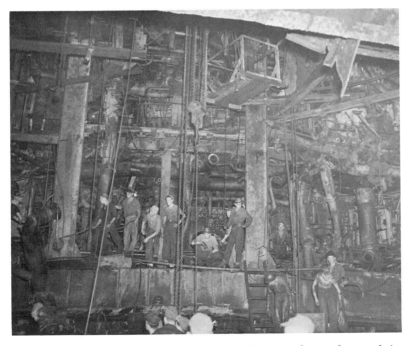

This view of the *Houston*'s forward engine room shows the crack in the vertical keel at frame 74½. It left the cruiser with a broken back, vulnerable to the ravages of inclement weather.

This is a close-up of the crack in the vertical keel at frame 74½.

bulkhead still appeared to have supported both the bottom and the inner bottom of the ship. Furthermore, it seemed to have restrained the distortion of the shell aft of that point, for observers in the dry dock could see an abrupt change in the contour of the ship's bottom plating at bulkhead 79.

Bulkhead 69—which was roughly eight feet farther away from the point of impact—was not damaged as extensively, even though it had been distorted badly enough to permit uncontrollable flooding of the forward fireroom. The keel was hogged upward into an arch of about 14 inches at frame 74. The vertical keel, made of 0.75-inch medium steel, had been cracked at frame 74½ and pulled apart by roughly an inch. The hull plating of the ship was wrinkled around her girth, all the way to the bottom of the portside armor belt. A number of cracks appeared in the shell plating. Under the after fireroom the bottom was dished in from two to three feet on the starboard side.

The opening in the ship's shell, in way of the after torpedo

Dry-docking at Manus reveals extensive damage to the *Houston*'s stern and rudder. A temporary patch, installed in Ulithi, covers part of the hole from the top to lessen the sea's pressure on the hangar's forward bulkheads.

The *Houston*'s portside hull as well as her main deck plating suffers from localized wrinkling.

hit, was approximately 32 feet long by 28 feet high. The main deck at the fantail had been torn loose from the shell plating and pushed upward by about four feet. The shell had wrinkled on the port side and in the main deck plating. With this evidence finally available, Miller was able to start some of the detailed calculations that would go into the *Houston*'s official damage report.

While he was doing this, the repair gangs began the task of removing twisted wreckage from the torpedo holes to create more working space. As the holes were gradually cleared, the repair gangs rigged chain falls to lower the damaged turbines, the reduction gear, and other heavy pieces of machinery through the hole in the hull to the bottom of the dry dock.

Lieutenant York was anxious to get this job done. Before the chain falls had been rigged to the high-pressure turbine, he told Shipfitter Harold Hurd to begin cutting the pipes that held it in place. Hurd had not progressed very far when the turbine gave its first ominous lurch. He turned off his torch and reported to York, who ordered him to cut a little more. York watched Hurd over his shoulder. The turbine lurched again, to everyone's alarm. This time the shipfitter was told to stop cutting the pipes until the chain falls could be hooked up. It was no use pressing their luck.[3] That hole in the bottom was big enough already.

CHAPTER FOURTEEN

Ready for Sea

After the initial damage surveys had been completed and the wreckage had been cleared away from the massive torpedo hole, the midships repair gang constructed the frame for a hull patch, according to York's plan. Shipfitter Hurd and the others built "T" beams, half an inch thick and three feet high, with tops that were an inch thick and a foot wide. These beams, spaced four feet apart, ran fore and aft, with spacer ribs—eight inches apart—between them. Since there was no way to bend or otherwise form the metal to follow the contour of the ship, the frame was emplaced straight and flat. Its outside edges were then trimmed to conform to the curve of the hull, as York had envisioned. Three major hull plates, roughly eight feet high by twenty-eight feet long, ran from the keel up to the armored belt and constituted most of the patch. Forward of these three main plates several uneven pieces three to four feet long were used to extend the patch to the original shell. The uneven pieces used aft of the main plates had to be eight to nine feet long.[1]

Since the *Houston*'s keel had been bowed upward for a length of about twenty feet by the first torpedo hit, the repair gang had trouble attaching the new side plating to the keel.

Eighteen days after the *Houston* is dry-docked at Manus, new longitudinals and transverse intercostals are placed in the hole amidships.

By the second week of February 1945, the midships hull patch is complete. It consists of three major plates, roughly 8 feet high by 28 feet long, and several uneven pieces used to extend the patch to the ship's original shell. Distortion in the *Houston*'s keel and hull can still be seen between frame 70 (where water is being discharged) and frame 79 (the bulge at the after end of the patch).

They decided to try brute force. After they had welded the plating to the new frame, they placed a hydraulic jack on the dry dock's keel blocks and used the jack to bend the plating and the frame up to meet the distorted keel.

Aside from hull repairs the major emphasis at Manus was on restoring the *Houston*'s ability to steam under her own power. Some of the machinery was damaged beyond repair and could only be discarded as scrap. Enough could be reconditioned, however, to place the no. 1, 2, and 4 boilers and the no. 2 and 3 main engines in operation. The reconditioning of the no. 2 and 4 boilers followed the pattern that had worked in restoring the no. 1 boiler prior to departure from Ulithi. The reconditioning of the no. 2 main engine began early, in Ulithi, even though the engine could not be tested or the job completed until the *Houston* reached the floating dry dock.

As soon as the water level in the after engine room had been lowered to the point where it no longer covered the upper gratings, repair gangs washed down the exposed surfaces of all machinery with hot salt water. The sooner they freed these surfaces from corrosive elements, the more they improved their chances of restoring the machinery to normal operation. Next they removed all gauges and thermometers from the no. 2 main unit and delivered them to the repair ship *Hector* for reconditioning.

They inspected the no. 2 reduction gear, finding some rust on the pinions and gears but no serious corrosion. Since the reduction gear had to be jacked up before they could work on it any further, the repair gangs had to wait two more days for the compartment to be pumped completely dry. Once they had raised the reduction gear and removed debris from around it, they were able to open the inspection plates of the turbines and the exhaust trunk. There appeared to be active corrosion on the low-pressure turbine rotor drum.

The repair gangs flushed both the low- and high-pressure turbines thoroughly with fresh water, then sprayed a preservative into each turbine through the inspection plates and the ahead and astern steam lines. The preservative formed a vapor that settled and condensed on all the interior parts.

Next the lubricating oil sump of the reduction gear was pumped out, cleaned, and wiped dry. A shortage of fresh water prevented the repair gang from flushing the sump at this time. They placed enough preservative in the sump to provide suction to the lubricating oil pump, and then they coupled an air drill to the jacking gear. Using two large-capacity gasoline-driven air compressors, they were able to rotate the turbine and operate the pump. This permitted a thorough inspection of the reduction gears, which revealed more rust.

After the rust had been stoned from the gears, the repair gang pumped the preservative from the system into a settling tank. They placed 200 gallons of lubricating oil into the system and pumped it through for two hours before finally pumping it overboard. Next they cleaned the strainers and placed 400 gallons of lubricating oil into the system.

With the lubricating system, including the purifier, thus in operation, the repair gang slowly rotated the turbine again. The strainers and the purifier would have to be cleaned frequently until all signs of rust and foreign matter were removed.

For six weeks the reduction gear was jacked for at least one hour each day to permit work on the turbines. When the repair gang removed the carbon packing from both the high-pressure and the low-pressure turbines, the rotor shafts underneath were found to be rusted and pitted. They would have to be cleaned, then stoned. It was tedious work, but eventually all the rust was removed, though some pitting remained. Next the repair gang sprayed the turbines with grade 3 Tectyl and painted the shafts with the heavier grade 1 Tectyl. They cleaned the carbon packing and put it in storage, where it would await engine testing.

The no. 3 and 4 main engines received essentially the same treatment, but the no. 4 was in extremely poor condition. It had been knocked out of alignment by the first torpedo hit and remained totally immersed for eighty-five days, until the forward engine room could be dewatered in Manus. The repair gang disconnected the no. 4 unit from its shafting and removed its propellor. Although it could not be used for the return voyage to the United States, careful treatment during that trip would permit it to be reconditioned and reinstalled in due course.

The propellor from the no. 1 main unit was removed early in the dry dock period. Its power unit was a wreck.

During the *Houston*'s day, if a cruiser took a torpedo hit in way of any machinery space other than the most forward fireroom, damage to at least one of her four shafts was inevitable. How badly the shafting was displaced depended upon the point of impact. In the *Houston*'s case the first torpedo hit came directly beneath the propelling machinery for the no. 1 shaft, which was the outboard shaft on the starboard side. The blast blew the low-pressure turbine against the armored third deck with enough force to open seams and cause extensive flooding on that level. The no. 1 shaft itself was broken at the coupling abaft the reduction gear, and the subsequent drag of the propellor pulled the entire shaft about five and a half feet toward the stern. The shaft came to rest with the forward coupling slightly aft of bulkhead 79 and about three feet above the normal shaft line. The forward pedestal bearing of the no. 1 shaft, at frame 83 in the after fireroom, was raised about three feet by the upward distortion of the bottom, which was noted during the first inspection after the *Houston* entered dry dock. The pedestal bearing remained reasonably intact, though little else did.

The no. 1 main unit was so badly damaged that the high-pressure turbine and the main condenser had to be scrapped. The low-pressure turbine casing was also scrapped, but the rotor and diaphragms were saved for reconditioning. The reduction gear was eventually shipped to the Mare Island Navy Yard for salvage. The shock of the torpedo hit had broken off several oil spray nozzles, and these had damaged the gear teeth.

As Shipfitter Hurd discovered when he first tried to cut loose the high-pressure turbine, removing the major pieces of machinery from the no. 1 engine was a hazardous task. A number of these heavy pieces were adrift; they threatened to fall through the large torpedo hole in the bottom of the shell and crash into the dry dock below.

Lieutenant York decided to suspend this machinery from the third deck with chain falls while the hull was being cut away between frames 70 and 79 in preparation for the installation of the new framework and side plating. This turned out to be a difficult rigging job, but the repair gang—undoubtedly motivated by visions of machinery falling on innocents below—accomplished it quickly.

The hull repair work proceeded through the remainder of January and into February. York and his contingent, mostly *Houston* men, concentrated on the work amidships; the Sea-Bees focused their efforts on the damaged stern, which included the removal and repair of the ship's rudder. A quick inspection revealed the reason for the *Houston*'s erratic behavior under tow, especially after the second torpedo hit. The rudder had been bent into a semicircle 20 degrees off center.

York and his people worked carefully to make their large patch watertight and structurally strong. The welders had to take pains to work slowly but not too long in the same place, for they had to give the welding area a chance to cool down periodically. Thus they avoided the heat strain that makes side plating vulnerable to buckling. They also dissipated heat strain by peening the new welds while the bead was still hot. The welders would start in the center of each patch and work outward, saving the edges for last. Finally, to ensure watertight integrity, they bolted the forward edge of each patch to the hull.

A special problem was posed by loose rivets that were causing oil leaks. There were three options for repair: the rivets could be caulked, welded in place, or removed and replaced with plugs. York chose the welding option, even though with it came the danger of fire or explosion. He worked around the problem by instructing his welders to strike an arc on top of the rivet. This would expand the rivet, thus effectively sealing

These sequential views (here and the following pages) show the progress of work done on the *Houston*'s damaged stern section within
weeks of entering dry dock. This photo was taken five days after entering dry dock.

Eight days after entering dry dock.

Two weeks after entering dry dock.

Repairs to the damaged stern and rudder are nearly complete by 15 February 1945.

the leak and eliminating the dangerous possibility of oil seep-age during later welding. After a short wait the rivet could be welded to the hull safely.

As the days in dry dock turned into weeks, a subtle change in mood began to appear. The crew of the *Houston* no longer regarded themselves as survivors but rather as members of the crew of a major combatant. The worst of their shared ordeal was now behind them. Much hard work remained, but they had come through, and they were going home.

The deck divisions gradually resumed their normal routines. They cleaned up their sections of the ship, repainted where they could, and taught new crew members their duties. Topside structures, undamaged hull areas, and weather decks regained a shipshape appearance. Captain Behrens had no intention of returning to the United States in a ship that looked like a candidate for the junkyard.

As work continued, occasional liberty parties found their way to the beaches and limited recreation facilities ashore. A fortunate few even managed to take short periods of leave in Australia. Many declined, however. They were reluctant to be listed among those who could be spared.

Shortly after the *Houston* entered dry dock, a number of SeaBees and other repair specialists reported on board for temporary duty. After a while the ship began to receive a different kind of newcomer—one who reported on board for transportation to the United States. This was an added strain for the *Houston*'s officers, who would be responsible for their safety.

Despite the threats of Tokyo Rose and the ominous portent of the air-raid alert the day the *Houston* went into dry dock, work on the ship proceeded without harassment except for one brief alert late in January. In this respect Manus proved to be much better than Ulithi. A generally optimistic mood now prevailed, with the midships patch nearly complete and the prospect of undocking less than a week distant.

Commander Miller was too tired to share in the fresh surge of optimism, although he admitted that repairs were generally going well. He had been caught up in the exhausting effort for months, trying to be everywhere and to check on everything around the clock. He realized that the unrelieved stress was probably bad for him and allowed himself infrequent breaks on the beach. But the monkey always went along.

Around sundown on 5 February Miller was down in the forward engine room bottoms watching York and his welders put a plate over the final hole in the hull, a section little more than a foot square. They heard a sudden commotion on the decks above. Hatches were slamming shut. Men were running for their battle stations. General quarters. FLASH BLUE. York continued welding. If the attack materialized they would have to flood the dry dock to minimize potential bomb damage. The water would come pushing up through that lousy little one-foot hole and wipe out weeks of work, at best. Miller didn't want to think of the worst case, another bomb or torpedo hit.

York kept on welding, totally absorbed in his work. Miller moved closer, where he could see over York's shoulder. How could he tell a man to weld faster? Miller bit his tongue and tried not to breathe loudly. The welding continued, but time had stopped. Nothing seemed to be happening. Finally word filtered down: "All clear."

The final week in dry dock moved quickly as the main machinery went through the final stages of reconditioning. On 11 February Miller formed a hull board, consisting of Lieutenant Commander Hibschman and Lieutenants Smith and York, to give the ship a final inspection before undocking. The inspection took all day. The four men scrutinized the hull and the underwater fittings; the inner bottoms; the vertical bulkheads of the boiler compartments; the underwater valves; the propellors and shafting; the rudder; and the power and hand pumps. They worked until 2230 that night. The *Houston* was ready to sail.

But there was always something else to detain them. Less than one hour after the inspection was completed a fire broke out in a third-deck compartment—somewhat unexpectedly,

On 12 February 1945 the *Houston* is undocked at Manus and readied to commence sea trials under her own power. Despite a fresh camouflage paint job, her port side amidships still shows the effects of repeated battering by the *Hector*'s shallow-draft camels in Ulithi, as well as extensive wrinkling aft from the second torpedo hit.

considering Schnable's excellent track record as fire chief during the dry dock period. The *Houston* went to fire quarters, and a fire-fighting party had the blaze out in nine minutes.

Preparations for getting under way continued through the night. At 0400 the no. 4 boiler was cut in on the main steam line. Two hours later the *Houston* ceased receiving steam and electricity from the dock. At 0700 flooding in the dry dock began. Within three hours the *Houston* was finally waterborne again, with a reasonably intact hull. The *Reno* was the first of the two cruisers to clear the floating dry dock. The *Houston* followed, towed by a dry dock tug.

After she emerged bow first from the dry dock, it took the *Houston* slightly more than an hour to reach her temporary anchorage. There she spent the afternoon testing her steering gear and her main engine units before halting tests to take on fuel. Even after receiving more than one hundred thousand gallons of fuel, the *Houston*'s mean draft was 21 feet, 7 inches— 10 feet less than it had been when she carried so much floodwater amidships.

The next day the *Houston* received another large draft of men who had been awaiting transportation to the United States and said good-bye to the final contingent of SeaBees who had been working on her. Tests of the various ship's systems continued to be run in preparation for the next day's post-repair sea trials.

On Wednesday, 14 February—four months to the day after receiving her first torpedo hit—the *Houston* was once again under way using her own power. Steaming outside Seeadler Harbor, she spent the day testing her propulsive machinery and making speed calibrations; she attained a speed of 23 knots on her two engines at 260 shaft revolutions per minute. She test-fired her 20mm antiaircraft guns. Everything was working well.

The *Houston* returned to her anchorage in Seeadler Harbor at dusk. Only one more day before she started home.

CHAPTER FIFTEEN

Homeward Bound

The final day in Manus seemed to drag on forever. After racing against the clock for the past four months, the crew of the *Houston* found themselves without much to do. Comparatively speaking, anyway. A final draft of homeward-bound men reported on board, swelling the passenger count to more than half the size that the crew was at the time of the first torpedoing. In mid-afternoon the *Houston* topped off her fuel tanks, taking on board another fifty-eight thousand gallons. Her mean draft was now 23 feet. She was ready to go.

At 0500 on Friday, 16 February, the *Houston* lighted fires under boilers no. 1 and 4, set material condition BAKER and readiness condition III, and set her special sea detail. By 0750 she was standing out of the Seeadler Harbor channel, fifteen minutes behind the *Reno*. Once clear of the antisubmarine net at the entrance to the channel, the two light cruisers made a rendezvous with the destroyer escort *Bowers* a half hour later.

The *Bowers* had been designated as the antisubmarine screen for the three-ship formation, Task Unit 72.6.11. Captain Behrens served as officer in tactical command. They settled into an average speed of advance in the 16-knot range, adopting an intermittent pattern of zigzagging to complicate the efforts of any trailing Japanese submarine skipper.

The prospect of either air, surface, or subsurface enemy contact diminished with each passing hour, however. They were quickly moving out of range of the Japanese. From this point on, the *Houston* would go to general quarters only for drill.

Still, this was not a pleasure cruise. For all her careful patch work and new buoyancy, the *Houston* was still a ship with a broken back, no match for a heavy sea. Even her moderate speed of advance, only two-thirds the speed she attained in her post-dry-dock trials, created stresses and reopened leaks frequently enough to keep the damage control teams busy. The ship required constant vigilance.

The men who had endured the four-month struggle to keep the *Houston* afloat were exhausted. Many, already pushed beyond the limit, were quietly transferred for long rests and psychiatric care. Others would go as the accumulated pressures of the situation continued to take their toll.

With the ship out of danger there was a new task to be performed. The *Houston* had to be fully transformed from a barely surviving hulk to a first-class ship of the line. This called for a new attitude on the part of the crew, who had become accustomed to mutilating the ship in order to save her. It meant a tight new shipboard organization under the division officers rather than one based on the survival requirements of damage control, messing, and sanitation. It meant a new emphasis on cleanliness and maintenance, which translated into a great deal of manual labor. Captain Behrens and Commander Broussard roamed throughout the ship, inspecting, instructing, counseling.

The *Houston* no longer had her formidable fighting capabilities, but the fighting pride of her crew had to be restored as the first order of business.

After four days at sea the formation neared Majuro Atoll, where the *Reno* and the *Bowers* were detached and Task Unit 72.6.11 was dissolved. Now the *Houston* was alone at sea for the first time in her short life. She plowed at a resolute 18 knots toward Pearl Harbor.

One day later, 21 February, she crossed the international date line. The *Houston* was back in home waters.

The next landfall came on Saturday morning, 24 February. At 0610 lookouts sighted Mount Heleakala on Maui Island, forty miles away. They had reached the Hawaiian chain. Three hours later the *Houston* reached the entrance to Pearl Harbor but faced an hour's wait while the carrier *Intrepid* was maneuvered into port. The crew was getting restless.

When it was the *Houston*'s turn, she picked up a pilot at the harbor entrance buoy, then passed through the antisubmarine net and moved through the narrow channel into the main harbor. Two yard tugs moved out to assist her into berth H4, where she was moored by 1047. Shortly afterwards the destroyer escort *Tills* was moored alongside to provide electrical power to the *Houston*, whose boiler fires had been left to die out.

Two hours later there was a sizeable exodus from the ship when a large draft of passengers departed, bound for the naval receiving station at Pearl Harbor. The crew of the *Houston* was not far behind them, ready to succumb to the blandishments of Honolulu on a Saturday night. Contrary to the expectations of some, the first night of real liberty since the preceding summer did not turn out to be a combination of New Year's Eve and Mardi Gras. Perhaps Honolulu was too big. Perhaps the shore patrol was too efficient. Or perhaps the crew was too tired. More likely, no one wanted to borrow trouble and get left behind when the *Houston* departed for the mainland in three days.

At any rate, their reentry into civilization was tame, and the next morning's muster on board the *Houston* produced no absentees or late arrivals. Only one man, in fact, earned the distinction of being returned to the ship by the shore patrol before liberty expired. He was Machinist's Mate Second Redford, the last man to be pulled from the escape trunk leading away from the flooded after fireroom. Redford had evidently needed to let off steam—he was charged with assault and battery and malicious injury.

The stop in Hawaii saw more reunions with former shipmates. A thirty-three-man marine detachment led by Captain O'Connor and Sergeant Harris returned to the *Houston*, which made it appear as if things were getting back to normal.

The three days in Pearl Harbor also provided opportunities for Commander Miller and the damage control gangs. Even though the weather and seas en route to Hawaii had been moderate, the working of the ship around her broken keel had produced a total of twenty-three cracks in the temporary "T"-beam longitudinals that had been installed in Ulithi. Most of these were at welded joints, and all could be repaired at Pearl Harbor. The lesson was clear: Any seas but the most gentle could place the *Houston* in jeopardy, and rather quickly. Beneath the facade of normalcy, real danger still lurked.

The growing realization that the *Houston* was still far from well had disturbing implications with respect to the crew's attitude toward their ship. If worsening conditions reimposed a salvage mentality, in which pride in good order and discipline might once again be subordinated to the overriding task of saving the ship, then the command effort of the past several weeks would be blunted. The crew was on its way back to civilization. A sailor lying in his bunk who wanted more fresh air could no longer reach up and cut a hole in the ventilation duct that ran overhead. A few weeks before it wouldn't have mattered. Now, it did. The ship-keeping frame of mind had been regenerated and it had to be preserved.

At least the carefully constructed bottom patches were holding firm. This was a real tribute to the skill of the SeaBees and of Lieutenant York's welders. Only a few minor leaks appeared below decks, and these were still more of a nuisance than a danger. Moreover, the *Houston* was not adding to her structural difficulties by carrying a great amount of floodwater.

At noon on 27 February the *Houston* was under way—once again in company with the *Reno*, which had rejoined her at Pearl Harbor. This time their destination was San Pedro, California.

With the sighting of South Point Light at 2100 on 5 March,

the two cruisers made a landfall thirty-three miles off of California's Santa Rosa Island.

During the night the *Reno* reported a submerged sonar contact. The watchstanders on the *Houston* were incredulous. Even Tokyo Rose couldn't dream this one up. It had to be a false alarm. It was.

At 0900 the next morning the *Houston* entered San Pedro Harbor and was moored portside to Net Pier at the naval operating base on Terminal Island. More former shipmates, including Firecontrolmen Joe Lilius and Jim Potter, reported back on board.

Lilius had a bizarre sea story to tell. He had last been seen wandering around the main deck of the *Houston* in a daze after the shock of the first torpedo hit had hurled him headfirst into an unyielding fixture. Seaman First Jim Bledsoe decided that Lilius needed a keeper and helped him over the side when the first order to abandon ship was given. But Lilius didn't remember this or anything about the next several days. The first thing he remembered after the hit was Bledsoe holding three fingers in front of his face and asking him how many there were.

Lilius had entered a time warp. As he looked around he recognized the SS *Dashing Wave*, a transport bound for the United States with a number of other *Houston* men. He had been in exactly the same situation before, even on board the same ship, after surviving the sinking of the cruiser *Helena* earlier in the war. Something was making him live through all his bad memories again, pushing him backward through time.

After a while Lulius' confusion lessened. His head cleared enough to form a gambling partnership with Bledsoe for the remainder of the trip back. Lilius specialized in blackjack and poker, Bledsoe in shooting craps. Their winnings were handsome. With part of them they bought a car when they reached the United States. They even managed to extract four brand-new tires from a harried ration board manager in El Paso.

Upon rejoining the *Houston*, Lilius requested permission

to drive his car across country and meet the ship in New York when she pulled into the Brooklyn Navy Yard for major repairs. With his bad memories of broken keels he had no desire to sail all the way to Brooklyn in a ship that had one. The first ship to be torpedoed out from under him, before the *Helena*'s demise, was the destroyer *Benham*, hit somewhere north of Guadalcanal in November 1942. He recalled vividly the moment that the *Benham*'s back broke. Her midsection rose above the forward and after sections. Then it plunged down and, just before the ship sank, her bow and stern shot high into the air.

Commander Broussard listened to Lilius' story with empathy but denied the request. The crew of the *Houston*, after all, belonged with the *Houston*.[1]

One cross-country trip was approved. Recently promoted Lieutenant Commander Julius Steuckert and Lieutenant A. C. Smith left the ship for temporary duty at the Brooklyn Navy Yard. They carried detailed damage estimates so that the extent of repair work could be calculated well before the damaged cruiser's arrival at the yard.

Steuckert had spent a lot of time on the project, making careful sketches on a set of the *Houston*'s plans to indicate the location of all rents and wrinkles, damaged strength members, and distorted bulkheads. The main purpose of this preparatory effort was to give the navy yard enough information to prefabricate replacements for many of the damaged sections of the *Houston* and thus save the time required for repair.

After he arrived in New York Steuckert was pleased to learn that the project officer for the *Houston*'s repair effort was one of his classmates from the Naval Academy. The project officer paid close attention as they went over the annotated plans together. Later, after the *Houston* arrived in New York and the plans could be checked against the actual damage, he made a special point of congratulating Steuckert on the accuracy of his sketches. But, he confided, very few replacements had been prefabricated, for the staff of ship constructors at the navy yard had regarded the sketches as exaggerations. Experience and common sense told them that no ship could have sustained such damage and remained afloat.[2]

The *Houston* was under way from San Pedro on 10 March, once again in company with the *Reno*. Their next stop would be the Panama Canal Zone. At Balboa a week later divers checked the *Houston*'s hull for four hours and reported that the patches amidships and on the stern were holding well. This was encouraging news, but the structural weakness of the ship, represented by the heavily cracked "T"-bar longitudinals, was still a major concern.

The ship's delicate condition finally precipitated a decision once she had cleared the Panama Canal the following day: She would stand out from Cristobal for New York via the Yucatan and Florida straits to avoid the Windward Passage, where she would be subject to the continuous pounding of head seas.

Shortly before midnight on 21 March, three days after transiting the canal, the *Reno* detached herself from the two-ship formation and proceeded into the Charleston Navy Yard. The *Houston* continued on course for New York. Two hours later her generators lost their electrical load. She lost steering control and went dead in the water. It was eerily reminiscent of the first torpedo attack. This time, however, the electrical casualty was quickly corrected and power was restored within ten minutes.

They were now less than two days out of New York. High winds and heavy seas were the *Houston*'s only worries now, and the weather forecast boded well. But Commander Miller, thinking ahead, found new cause for concern.

The *Houston* would have to pass under the Brooklyn Bridge moments before arriving at her final destination. Normally, clearance between the cruiser's topmast and the lowest girder of the bridge would not have been a problem. But the *Houston* was not a normal ship any more. She was missing her no. 1 and no. 4 main engines, several oil and ballast tanks, sizeable portions of her superstructure, and a great deal of other topside weight that had been jettisoned in her fight for survival. She was riding a couple of feet higher in the water than when she first went to war. What if the *Houston* lost her topmast to the bridge just as she made her triumphal entry into the Brooklyn Navy Yard?

Miller began making some close calculations, reworking his figures as new information became available: the tidal state at the exact moment the *Houston* passed under the bridge; the amount of fuel left in the tanks; the change in average draft of the ship as fuel consumption continued. The figures looked good. He would have a little room to spare. To be on the safe side, however, he checked and tested the remaining ballasting pumps. They were in good shape to help lower the *Houston*'s draft if things started going wrong.

At 0920 on Friday, 23 March—five weeks after she left Manus—the *Houston* entered New York Harbor's mine-cleared entrance channel. By 1145 she was anchored in five fathoms of water in Gravesend Bay, ready to offload fuel and ammunition to barges that came alongside. The removal of this material further lessened the ship's draft and sent Miller back to his slide rule.

The next morning the cruiser began her final brief journey to pier D, berth 5, in the navy yard. Miller stationed himself on the forecastle to monitor the passage under the Brooklyn Bridge. He was taking no chances. He ordered the engineers to increase ballast. As they approached the bridge, it seemed to get lower and lower. Something told him that this was just an optical illusion, that overhead structures always look lower from the surface of the water than they really are.

Miller involuntarily hunched his shoulders as the topmast passed under the bridge—safely. Perhaps they had cleared by inches. Perhaps by feet. He would never know. The monkey pouted.

The *Houston* tied up at pier D, once again to await her turn for entry into dry dock. It was all over. An odyssey of fourteen thousand miles. And not one of those miles had been easy.

Back in the western Pacific, the *Houston*'s running mates

were assembling for the imminent invasion of Okinawa. To counteract the mighty American armada, Japanese defenders were readying a final trump card—the kamikazes, whose devastating attacks on American shipping would ultimately cost the navy more casualties in the bloody Okinawa campaign than the army and the marines combined.

The crew of the *Houston* was already trying to expedite repairs so she could get back in the war. But it was ending, faster than anyone expected. Within a month the war in Europe would be over and the American president who had taken such a personal interest in both *Houston* cruisers would be dead. Events would continue to accelerate over the succeeding four months until Japan lay defeated and the world had crossed the threshold of an uncertain new nuclear age.

At war's end the *Houston*'s yard work was two months shy of completion. Even after V-J day workmen swarmed over the dry-docked ship, almost oblivious to the crew. From turret no. 4 aft they designed and welded on a new stern to replace the patchwork of twisted metal and temporary bulkheads whose only practical function had been to keep the water out. New main machinery was going in, along with a great deal of new electrical work. Simultaneously, the yard workers were restoring the ship's structural strength by rebuilding her virtually from the keel up.

The *Houston* lay in dry dock like a patient on an operating table. Her decks were festooned with air and fire hoses and electrical cables. Oxygen and acetylene bottles and fire extinguishers were everywhere. The din of chipping and riveting was continuous and pervasive, and it made normal conversation impossible.

Adding to the confusion was a devastating loss of personnel. The number of new men that normally join a ship when she's in a navy yard was cut by the sudden end of the war, and many experienced officers and enlisted men were hastily released from active duty. The crew as well as the ship would have to be rebuilt from the keel up.

The *Houston*'s change-of-command ceremony on 30 July 1945 draws a number of casual though interested spectators at the Brooklyn Navy Yard. Having assumed command from Captain Behrens, Captain Howard E. Orem addresses the crew for the first time.

Following the departure of Commander Broussard, Commander Cook served as executive officer before the assignment passed to Commander Miller. Shortly afterwards, on 30 July, Captain Behrens relinquished his command to Captain Howard E. Orem.

Captain Orem brought a fine service reputation with him to the *Houston*. He had capped extensive service in battleships, carriers, cruisers, and destroyers with a demanding stint as executive assistant to the wartime commander in chief of the navy, Admiral Ernest J. King. The new commanding officer quickly recognized the need—and the opportunity—to rebuild the crew along with the ship. His attention to detail was constructive and instructive. His quiet self-confidence was inspirational, and his determination never to be defeated was something that Miller would not forget.

On 11 October 1945 the *Houston*, now rebuilt at a fraction (five million dollars) of her original cost (thirty-six million), steamed out of New York Harbor for a shakedown cruise and refresher training at Guantanamo Bay, Cuba. Barely a dozen crew members remained of those who had shared the ordeal off Formosa almost a year earlier. No one knew it at the time, but the cruiser had little more than two years of active service remaining.

Her training in the Caribbean was interrupted by a heartwarming return to the city of Houston. She was there on Navy Day, 27 October 1945, a year to the day from her arrival, under tow, at Ulithi. After the celebration she returned to the Caribbean to complete refresher training, then sailed back to New York in time for Christmas. She moved to Newport, Rhode Island, in January 1946. In mid-April she was assigned to temporary duty with the Twelfth Fleet as flagship for Admiral H. Kent Hewitt, commander of U.S. naval forces in Europe. Between May and December the cruiser visited thirty-two ports, operating in the Baltic and North seas, the eastern Atlantic, and the Mediterranean. Early in that period Captain Neil K.

Dietrich relieved Captain Orem as the commanding officer. In December 1946 the *Houston* returned to New York for the holidays. The following month she departed once again for Newport, where command passed to Captain Kenmore M. McManes on 30 January 1947.

After extensive training in the Caribbean the *Houston* made her final transatlantic cruise, then began preparations for inactivation. She was placed out of commission and in reserve on 15 December 1947, four years and five days after she was commissioned. The *Houston* was stricken from the navy list on 1 March 1959.

Epilogue

When the city fathers of Houston, Texas, received word that their ship was repaired and ready for sea, they moved quickly. Enough time remained for them to plan for the cruiser to visit Houston on Navy Day, 27 October. The deal was on.

Leaving the Caribbean, the crew readied the *Houston* for her homecoming visit to Texas. As many drills and exercises were crowded in as possible, because a substantial part of the crew had reported on board directly from recruit training centers.

On 25 October the *Houston* anchored off Galveston, Texas, and took on board one hundred members of the crew of her predecessor, the heavy cruiser *Houston* (CA 30). These men, recently rescued from their Asian prison camps, had been invited by the Navy Department to interrupt their ninety-day leave periods to take part in the Houston Navy Day celebration.

The following morning the *Houston* steamed slowly upstream through the Houston ship channel in a procession that included three submarines, two destroyers, and a destroyer escort, all veterans of the Pacific War. Crowds gathered along the banks of the channel. Sailors on deck waved to their audience, who returned the salutation with handkerchiefs and small flags. It was a holiday scene, a time for cheering in the bright morning sunshine. As the cruiser passed the San Jacinto battle-ground, a squadron of naval aircraft flew overhead in formation.[1]

The cruiser moved through the channel, and Commander Miller broadcast a short radio message relayed by a commercial station to the citizens of Houston thanking them for their support and their invitation to the city. In the channel a great number and variety of ships and craft lay to and rendered passing salutes. The *Houston* was finally docked in the turning basin, five miles from downtown.

Mayor Otis Massey greeted Captain Orem as the big ship was warped in by tugs. The mayor had joined the *Houston* in Guantanamo, together with Chamber of Commerce president George Sawtelle, Navy League president George Brown, and Claud Hamill, chairman of the 1942 war loan drive that had funded the ship.

Over the next several days more than fifty thousand residents of the city and neighboring areas would visit the *Houston* and her dockside exhibits.

On Navy Day the official round of ceremonies started. Newly promoted Commodore Behrens spoke in the Palmer Memorial Church at 1000 for the formal commissioning of the Rice Institute naval reserve officers training corps unit. Later, at 1100, Mayor Massey and the members of the city council led a moving and dramatic welcoming ceremony on the steps of Houston's city hall. Commodore Behrens was the first to respond to their greetings and congratulations, in behalf of all those who had sailed with him. Captain Orem spoke for the current crew of the *Houston*, whose young faces revealed both pleasure and bewilderment at being in the center of so much attention.[2]

A special outpouring of sentiment greeted the survivors of the CL 81's predecessor, the heavy cruiser *Houston* (CA 30), some of whom had enjoyed the city's hospitality on earlier port visits. After one night in town the size of their contingent shrank noticeably. The chief master-at-arms, charged with taking daily muster, barely counted fifty present on the second morning. The next day he did not even bother counting. After all, these men were on their own leave time.[3]

After Mayor Massey dedicated a plaque to the memory of all those who had been lost from both cruisers, the town and the ship exchanged gifts. Then the entertainment, which had begun the previous evening, got rolling again. It would last for several days—receptions, parties, dances, the biggest of which took place in the city auditorium. A Mardi Gras spirit burst across the city, in vivid contrast to the despairing mood that had gripped the townspeople three years earlier. The long and bitter war was finally ending for them, too.

But the hardships of war would continue to exact their price, quietly, unseen. Early in his visit to Houston Commander Miller awakened to a frightening sensation in his hotel room downtown. His legs and arms were numb. He had felt something similar during the fire below decks on the way to Ulithi, and periodically since then in his hands and his feet, but he had always had something more urgent to worry about. And the symptoms had always gone away, until now.

He had to return to the ship in uniform. He dressed himself with great difficulty. The hardest part was working his way across the hotel lobby, using furniture for support. On board the *Houston* the ship's doctors were puzzled by the sudden onset of the affliction. They made a preliminary diagnosis of multiple sclerosis and recommended hospitalization ashore.

Miller did not want to leave the ship. He and his wife sought a second medical opinion. His brother, an army air corps colonel, traveled to Houston from his duty station in Florida to assist. Together they approached Captain Orem. Orem, who agreed that a second opinion was in order, permitted Miller to remain on board ship and serve as executive officer.

The search for a second opinion finally led to a neurologist who linked Miller's symptoms to some of those observed in victims of beriberi. He diagnosed Miller's condition as a severe deficiency of vitamin B_1, brought about by a year of continuous stress. The second opinion brought encouraging results. Massive daily doses of the vitamin eventually alleviated the symptoms somewhat. Miller began a therapy program, taking long, lonely walks about the decks late at night, when the crew was less apt to see how uncertainly he moved. By the following summer he had improved enough to leave the ship for duty at the Naval War College in Newport, thus vindicating Captain Orem's judgment.

A war had ended, and it was a time of new beginnings, both for a ship and for a man who had been severely scarred by that war. The wounds of each required careful tending and would require more, perhaps for a long time. Persistence and guts had prevailed. But at what cost?

Comments on the *Houston* Experience

Just prior to the *Houston*'s last cruise the Bureau of Ships completed a comprehensive war damage report. It credited the *Houston*'s damage control teams with saving the ship and paid special attention to the measures they employed during the forty-three hours that elapsed between the first and second torpedo hits. Without significant improvements made to the cruiser's stability and buoyancy during that period, she might never have survived the second hit and the subsequent tow to Ulithi, favorable weather or not.

A series of calculations demonstrated how fortunate the *Houston* had been to avoid heavy weather on her return trip to the United States. The profusion of floodwater and consequent sagging amidships had increased the bending moment at frame 75 by 54 percent. With this staggering increase in leverage, applied against the damaged keel, heavy weather would have pushed the ship past the point of disaster. It would have raised the tensile stress in the keel far above the yield strength of the steel and possibly beyond the steel's ultimate strength. Without a doubt the ship would have broken up, and rather quickly.

The bureau report praised the stiffeners that the *Houston*'s welders had fabricated and installed to reinforce buckled longitudinal beams. It noted that these repairs were the most extensive ever made under way by a ship's damage control teams during the war, and this despite extremely adverse conditions. Nevertheless, the strenuous stiffening efforts represented a potential reduction in the keel's tensile stress of only one percent with the ship in the worst hogging condition. Even the installation of new longitudinal strength members at Ulithi would have contributed only another four percent reduction under worst-case conditions. The extensive dewatering of compartments at Ulithi accounted for a potential stress reduction of an additional 16 percent, although two major compartments still remained totally flooded when the *Houston* departed from Ulithi.

The *Houston's* experience triggered some improvements throughout the navy in damage control capability. The most basic were increases in damage control equipment allowances for individual ships, higher-capacity pumps and welding equipment, and additional rescue breathing devices. There were changes in ship design as well. An additional fore-and-aft fire main was included on the second deck of the CA 139 and CL 144 classes of cruisers.

Such improvements in hardware aside, the *Houston's* experience raises some basic questions with respect to the survival of severely damaged ships. The gravest dangers that face any ship at sea are flooding and fire. The crew of the *Houston* had to contend with each. Neither flooding nor fire can be controlled from a distance. The damage control teams must close with them. But they must know what they are doing to fight such dangers at close quarters. This strongly suggests that every member of a ship's crew must be trained at the very minimum to take effective individual action promptly to control both flooding and fire.

In case of heavy battle damage, many of the crew may be released from combat and engineering stations that have been knocked out of action. They should be able to function as part of damage control teams in the more specialized work of shoring, pumping, or welding. A ship's damage control capability requires extensive training, which at times may conflict with the demands of operational training. It also calls for acute judgment in establishing priorities.

Long-service personnel tend to be more reliable in survival situations than those with limited time at sea. The limits of their performance are quickly reached, though, when they are repeatedly exposed to the hazards of ship abandonment. On board the *Houston*, some veterans of multiple torpedoings, like Machinist's Mate First Harrelson, appeared not to let their searing experience affect their performance. Far more commonplace was a susceptibility to the stresses of continual crises; for these men hope of saving the ship was quickly lost and individual survival became paramount. There was a tendency as well for less experienced hands to cluster around the older ones who had experience in abandoning ship. This, among other things, accounted for a rapid spread in the contagion of hopelessness.

As analysis subsequently bore out, no one on board the *Houston* had cause for unfettered optimism, and those assigned the task of keeping the ship afloat had the least. But it would have been impossible to carry on day after day without a certain measure of confidence. In time the *Houston*'s crew managed to regain some faith in their ship and in themselves, but only after several devastating periods in which despair showed clearly in their faces. Their hard-won confidence was a fragile thing that did not always stand up to repeated battering. Ultimately, however, it prevailed to save the ship.

The *Houston*'s experience raises a fundamental question concerning accountability of command at sea: When and how should abandon ship be ordered?

When the *Houston* was active, the abandonment and sinking of crippled ships was clearly favored, even in cases where they might have been saved. This policy was tactically expedient particularly in the earlier days of World War II, when the U.S. Navy did not dominate the seas. Thus Admiral Halsey's decisions to tow the *Canberra* and the *Houston* were contrary to the general drift of opinion in the navy. They were brave decisions that forced him to make significant adjustments in major battle plans; the option of towing had to be weighed against his primary mission at the time—that of supporting the landing at Leyte Gulf.

In the case of the *Houston* the willingness of the fleet commander to add to the towing formation already assembled for the *Canberra* was almost negated by a precipitate local decision to abandon ship. The decision, apparently driven less by the belief that the ship was breaking up than by doubt about her ability to withstand a long towing period, was made before actual conditions on board the damaged ship were carefully appraised.

The finality of an abandon-ship order will disrupt, very quickly, any serious efforts to keep the ship afloat. Under certain circumstances it will turn a marginal condition into an irreversibly disastrous one. The *Houston*'s abandon-ship procedures, with some exceptions, were generally handled in an orderly fashion, but the exodus of two-thirds of the crew took valuable skills and experience over the side. The loss of expertise was most immediately felt when the makeshift forecastle crew rigged for tow with the *Boston*.

The early order to abandon ship left those who were trying to save the *Houston* in a difficult position, risking charges of insubordination if they persisted. The *Houston*'s situation, however, did not have to call for decisions cast in stark either/or terms. Her experience suggests a need for carefully defined procedures for progressive abandonment in cases where sinking is not a foregone conclusion. Anyone whose task is not vital to the needs of an endangered ship should be free to go, but key personnel—officers, chief petty officers, damage control personnel, communicators—should remain with the captain to fight for the ship's survival as long as hope remains. On board the *Houston* such a procedure did evolve, but only in fits and starts and with a great deal of uncertainty.

A ship's abandonment throws the members of her crew into a life-threatening situation in which they must become suddenly and totally committed to self-preservation. In terms of its impact on the crew, then, the abandonment of a battle-damaged ship is analogous to a local act of surrender. It may differ in form but it does not differ in substance from a surrender of troops on land. Beyond the physical dimension—the certain loss of the ship and the possible loss of all or part of her crew—there is a psychological one. As the testimony of oft-torpedoed survivors shows, even the suggestion of abandonment is likely to erode the will to fight on. This, in turn, only intensifies the vulnerability of the crew, both to the enemy and to the sea. For this reason alone a commanding officer must remain no less accountable for a decision to abandon ship than he would for a grounding or a collision.

The rallying cry "Don't give up the ship!" still has meaning. For as long as any shred of hope exists for a fighting man, he must keep saying to himself, "I will not be defeated. No matter what the cost."

Notes

Prologue

Unless otherwise noted the material in the prologue is derived from "History of Ships Named *Houston*" (undated, ca. 1948 or later), Ships History, Naval Historical Center, Washington, D.C., and Samuel Eliot Morison, *History of United States Naval Operations in World War II*, vol. 3 (Boston: Atlantic–Little, Brown and Co., 1948).

1. William A. Kirkland in letter to author, 4 Aug 82.
2. Walter G. Winslow, *The Fleet the Gods Forgot* (Annapolis: Naval Institute Press, 1982), p. xi.
3. Ibid., p. 218.
4. W. Karig and W. Kelley, *Battle Report: Pearl Harbor to the Coral Sea* (New York: Farrar and Rinehart, Inc., 1944), p. 246.
5. Kirkland letter.
6. Chief of naval personnel in memo to secretary of the navy, 12 Oct 42, P-254-RMW, Ships History, Naval Historical Center, Washington, D.C.
7. H. M. Robertson, interview with author, San Francisco, 2 Oct 82.
8. *USS* Houston *[CL 81] Chronicle*, 27 Oct 45.
9. Chief of naval personnel in letter to David G. Richey, 26 Mar 43, P-254-RMW, Ships History Section, Naval Historical Center.
10. Kirkland letter.

Chapter One

Unless otherwise noted the material in this chapter is derived from "History of Ships Named *Houston*"; "History of USS *Houston* (CL 81)" (undated), Ships Data Section, Public Information Division, Office of Public Relations, Navy Department; Commanding officer, USS *Houston* (CL 81), letter, 11 Sep 47, CL-81/A12/KMM/M, 757, Ships History Section, Naval Historical Center; Newport News Shipbuilding and Dry Dock Company, "USS *Houston* in Epic Survival," *Shipyard Bulletin*, vol. 10, no. 11 (Sep 45): 10–13 and 32; and Rear Admiral George H. Miller, interview by John T. Mason, Feb 71, U.S. Naval Institute Oral History Collection, U.S. Naval Institute, Annapolis, Md., pp. 44–113.

1. *The Washington Star*, 20 Jun 43.
2. Mrs. I. B. McFarland in letter to secretary of the navy, 15 Jun 43, Ships History Section, Naval Historical Center.
3. Captain C. O. Cook in letter to author, 1 Aug 82.

Chapter Two

Unless otherwise noted the material in this chapter is derived from "History of Ships Named *Houston*"; "History of Houston"; Commanding officer, *Houston*, letter, 11 Sep 47; "Epic Survival"; Samuel Eliot Morison, *History of United States Naval Operations in World War II*, vol. 12 (Boston, Atlantic–Little, Brown and Co., 1948); Log book of the USS *Houston* (CL 81), 1–31 Oct 44, record group 24, Bureau of Personnel, National Archives; and Commanding officer, *Houston* (CL 81), letter to commander in chief, U.S. Fleet, 20 Oct 44, CL81/A16-3, serial 0134, Operational Archives, Naval Historical Center, Washington, D.C.

1. C. Vann Woodward, *The Battle For Leyte Gulf* (New York: Macmillan, 1947), p. 28.
2. Ibid., pp. 8, 16.
3. W. Karig, R. L. Harris, F. A. Manson, *Battle Report: The End of an Empire* (New York: Rinehart and Co., Inc., 1948), p. 323.
4. J. B. Lilius in letter to author, 20 Feb 83.

Chapter Three

Unless otherwise noted the material in this chapter is derived from "History of Ships Named *Houston*"; Ships Data Section, "History of *Houston*"; Commanding officer, *Houston*, letter, 11 Sep 47;

"Epic Survival"; *Houston* log, 1–31 Oct 44; Commanding officer, *Houston*, letter, 20 Oct 44; Miller interview; "Torpedo Damage Off Formosa—14 and 16 October 1944," BuShips damage report 53, 15 Mar 47, Bureau of Ships, Navy Department; and Lieutenant Commander W. A. Kirkland, letter to author, 12 Aug 82.

1. Lieutenant Commander W. A. Kirkland, statement in USS *Houston* file, ca. 1945, archives, Naval Historical Center, Washington, D.C.

2. Ibid.

3. H. M. Robertson in letter to author, ca. 1982.

4. Donald R. Smith in letter to author, 25 Aug 82.

5. Leslie M. Quay in letter to author, 15 Nov 81.

Chapter Four

Unless otherwise noted the material in this chapter is derived from Miller interview; "Torpedo Damage off Formosa"; and Byron S. Harris in letter to author, ca. 1982.

1. John J. Skarzenski in letter to author, 26 Jul 82.

2. John H. Rooney in letter to author, ca. 1982.

3. Captain William V. Pratt, in letter to author, 7 Jul 82.

4. H. M. Shafman in letter to author, ca. 1983.

5. Pratt letter.

6. Kirkland letter.

7. Ibid.

8. Allen Hayslett in letter to author, ca. 1982.

9. Lieutenant Commander W. A. Kirkland, informal report to commanding officer of *Houston* (undated), in letter to author, 12 Aug 82.

10. Anthony J. Caserta in letter to author, 14 Feb 82.

11. Potter letter.

12. Quay letter.

13. Lilius letter.

Chapter Five

Unless otherwise noted the material in this chapter is derived from Miller interview and *Houston* log, Oct 44.

1. Rooney letter.

2. Frank J. Campanella in letter to author, ca. 1982.

3. Hayslett letter.

4. Captain C. O. Cook in letter to author, 6 Nov 82.

5. Pratt letter.

Chapter Six

Unless otherwise noted the material in this chapter is derived from Morison, *United States Naval Operations*, vol. 12; Miller interview; *Houston* log, Oct 44; and "Torpedo Damage off Formosa."

1. Vann Woodward, *Leyte Gulf*, p. 19.

Chapter Seven

Unless otherwise noted the material in this chapter is derived from Morison, *United States Naval Operations*, vol. 12; Miller interview; *Houston* log, Oct 44; "Torpedo Damage off Formosa"; Commanding officer, *Houston* (CL 81), letter to commander in chief, U.S. Fleet, 29 Oct 44, CL81/A16-3, serial 0135; and William J. Miller, letter to author, 7 Jul 82.

1. Alex Macaw in letter to author, 15 Oct 82.

2. Rooney letter.

3. Richard S. Wolf in letter to author, 17 Jul 82.

4. Kirkland letter.

5. Campanella letter.

6. Lieutenant Commander W. A. Kirkland, informal report to commanding officer of *Houston* (undated, ca. 1944), in letter to author, 12 Aug 82.

7. Campanella letter.

8. Macaw letter.

9. Quay letter.

Chapter Eight

Unless otherwise noted the material in this chapter is derived from Miller interview; *Houston* log, Oct 44; and "Torpedo Damage off Formosa."

1. Morison, *United States Naval Operations*, vol. 12, p. 102.

2. Macaw letter.

3. Morison, *United States Naval Operations*, vol. 12, p. 102.

4. Ibid., p. 104.

5. Edwin P. Hoyt, *The Battle of Leyte Gulf: The Death Knell of the Japanese Fleet* (New York: Weybright and Talley, 1972), p. 27.

6. Vann Woodward, *Leyte Gulf*, p. 17.

7. Karig et al., *End Of An Empire*, p. 330.

8. Morison, *United States Naval Operations*, vol. 12, p. 108.

9. Ibid., p. 109.

Chapter Nine

Unless otherwise noted the material in this chapter is derived from Miller interview; *Houston* log, Oct 44; and "Torpedo Damage off Formosa."

1. Steuckert letter.

2. Capt C. O. Cook in letter to author, 1 Jan 83.

3. Ibid.

Chapter Ten

Unless otherwise noted the material in this chapter is derived from Miller interview; *Houston* log, Oct 44; and Rear Admiral Ralph James, interview by John T. Mason, Jr., 6 Apr 71, U.S. Naval Institute oral history collection, U.S. Naval Institute, Annapolis, Md., pp. 143–64.

1. Morison, *United States Naval Operations*, vol. 12, p. 109.

Chapter Eleven

Unless otherwise noted the material in this chapter is derived from Miller interview and *Houston* log, Oct 44 and Nov 44, record group 24, Bureau of Personnel, National Archives, Washington, D.C.

1. T. C. Wilbar in comments to author, Jan 84

2. James interview, p. 245.

3. Ibid., p. 146.

Chapter Twelve

Unless otherwise noted the material in this chapter is derived from Miller interview; *Houston* log, Nov and Dec 44, record group 24, Bureau of Personnel, National Archives, Washington, D.C.; and "Torpedo Damage off Formosa."

1. James interview, pp. 147–48.

2. Ibid., p. 147.

3. Harold E. Hurd in letter to author, 3 Dec 81.

4. John J. Seagraves in letter to author, 18 Jul 82.

Chapter Thirteen

Unless otherwise noted the material in this chapter is derived from Miller interview; *Houston* log, Dec 44 and Jan 45, record group 24, Bureau of Personnel, National Archives, Washington, D.C.; and "Torpedo Damage off Formosa."

1. C. C. York in letter to author, Aug 82.
2. Rooney letter.
3. Hurd letter.

Chapter Fourteen

Unless otherwise noted the material in this chapter is derived from Miller interview; *Houston* log, Jan and Feb 45, record group 24, Bureau of Personnel, National Archives, Washington, D.C.; and "Torpedo Damage off Formosa."

1. Hurd letter.

Chapter Fifteen

Unless otherwise noted the material in this chapter is derived from Miller interview and *Houston* log, Feb and Mar 45, record group 24, Bureau of Personnel, National Archives, Washington, D.C.

1. Lilius letter.
2. Steuckert letter.

Epilogue

Unless otherwise noted the material in the epilogue is derived from Miller interview; "Torpedo Damage off Formosa"; "History of Ships Named *Houston*"; Commanding officer, *Houston*, letter, Sep 47; and Rear Admiral George H. Miller, letter to author, 1983.

1. Jim Carroll, "Houston Gives Rousing Welcome to Cruiser," Houston *Press*, 26 Oct 45.
2. Ibid.
3. Kirkland letter.

Bibliographical Essay

In general, the official and unofficial source material relating to the ships named *Houston* fall into two distinct categories. Primary source material proves most useful in constructing a framework of the light cruiser *Houston*'s actions. Published secondary sources, on the other hand, provide valuable background material on the heavy cruiser *Houston*, the extraordinary response of Houstonians to her sinking, and their efforts to replace her. In addition, secondary sources help place the ordeal of the light cruiser *Houston* within both a strategic and a tactical context, highlighting the connections between Admiral Halsey's fleet-level decisions and the *Houston*'s ultimate fate.

A number of key primary source materials can be found in the operational archives branch of the Naval Historical Center in the Washington, D.C., Navy Yard. A central document is USS *Houston* (CL 81), "Torpedo Damage Off Formosa, 14 and 16 October 1944," war damage report no. 53, Bureau of Ships, 15 Mar 47. This report offers summaries of battle actions in which the light cruiser sustained damage; a detailed description of the damage and actions taken to contain and repair it; and analytical comments about the effectiveness of such actions. It also includes detailed sketches of the ship showing damaged and flooded areas. Another key report is the USS *Houston* war damage report, serial 001, 6 January 45. Prepared in Manus during the *Houston*'s dry-dock period, this document goes into extensive detail, evidently providing much of the data for the subsequent Bureau of

Ships report, and makes recommendations for improvements in ship design and for increased allowances of damage control equipment to be carried on board.

Two key battle reports are also filed in the navy's operational archives. The commanding officer, USS *Houston*, letter to commander in chief, U.S. Fleet, CL81/A16-3, serial 0134, 20 Oct 44, is a report of actions occurring on 12, 13, and 14 October 1944. It provides a detailed chronological summary of battle action through the evening of the first torpedoing and analyzes the effectiveness of the *Houston*'s fire discipline and fire control procedures as well as the performance of weapons and ordnance, both friendly and enemy. The document includes plotting board diagrams of task group dispositions; separate form reports for each action; and an analytical report from the *Houston*'s combat information center. Some preliminary damage assessments are included as well. Similar in format to the earlier battle report, the commanding officer, USS *Houston*, letter to commander in chief, U.S. Fleet, CL81/A16-3, serial 0135, 29 Oct 44, is relatively brief, because the 16 October action it describes was shorter. In addition to a description of the second torpedoing, this report outlines the changes made in shipboard antiaircraft defense organization after the first torpedo hit on 14 October.

Miscellaneous documents that can be found in the operational archives include monthly command summaries of action; copies of congratulatory messages from COMTHIRDFLT and others; rosters of personnel decorated for their courageous or meritorious actions; and summary statements by Captain W. W. Behrens, USN, and Lieutenant Commander W. A. Kirkland, USNR. These statements, though lacking the detail of the official reports, provide a colorful overview of the battle action and some insights into Captain Behrens's thinking about the *Houston*'s traumatic experience.

A basic reference paper, "History of Ships Named *Houston*" (undated, ca. 1948 or later), which provides chronological information on all three ships bearing that name, is located in the ships history branch of the Naval Historical Center. Miscellaneous letters and newspaper clippings pertaining to the renaming and launching of the light cruiser *Houston* are also on file there.

The National Archives in Washington, D.C., house the log books of the light cruiser *Houston* and the fleet tug *Pawnee* (ATF 74). These are particularly valuable records. They reconcile minor discrepancies of time and place in varied official and unofficial accounts of action; record times of air alerts, attacks, and other local actions; and provide detailed personnel information—gains, losses, injuries, deaths—often by name. However, the logs are almost totally lacking in analytical or interpretive detail and offer little in the way of battle action narrative.

The oral history collection at the U.S. Naval Institute in Annapolis contains two significant transcripts. The interview of Rear Admiral George H. Miller by John T. Mason, Feb 71, pp. 44–113, reveals Admiral Miller's insights and philosophy, which go to the heart of the *Houston*'s saga of survival and also form the basis for the questions raised in the epilogue. The interview of Rear Admiral Ralph James by John T. Mason, Mar 71, pp. 143–64, on the other hand, provides the best on-scene commentary from a noncrew member on the extent of the *Houston*'s battle damage. Admiral James, who was instrumental in running the navy's forward-based ship repair effort in the western Pacific during World War II, speaks of the *Houston*'s innovative damage control efforts from the perspective of an experienced ship constructor.

Finally, the subjective, qualitative side of the *Houston*'s experience—the heart and at times the conscience of the history—comes from the crew members themselves. Members of the USS *Houston* Association provided more than seventy-five responses to Admiral Miller's requests for personal recollections and related documentation. These responses ranged from one-page notes to full-blown unpublished essays and included rosters, newspaper clippings, copies of letters and memoranda (with two or more ship's histories, written earlier than the one on file at the Naval Historical Center), and detailed accounts of specific incidents. In the aggregate, this material yielded a wealth of information, both for fleshing out the official accounts and for cross-checking sea stories.

Leading the list of secondary sources are Morison's naval histories of World War II, written with the advantage of postwar hindsight and access to Japanese records. Four sources were consulted for background on the heavy cruiser *Houston*. Samuel Eliot Morison's *History of United States Naval Operations in World War II*, vol. 3 (Boston: Atlantic–Little, Brown and Company, 1948), reconciles as far as possible American accounts of the *Houston*'s sinking with Japanese records. A survivor of that sinking provides a dramatic firsthand account of the final days of the U.S. Asiatic Fleet in W. G. Winslow's *The Fleet the Gods Forgot* (Annapolis: Naval Institute Press, 1982). An Australian view of the final days of the ill-fated force of American, British, Dutch, and Australian warships in the southwest Pacific is presented by David Thomas in *The Battle of the Java Sea* (New York: Stein and Day, 1969). Finally, an early volume in the *Battle Report* series, W. Karig and W. Kelley, *Battle Report: Pearl Harbor to the Coral Sea* (New York: Farrar and Rhinehart, Inc., 1944) covers the loss of the heavy cruiser *Houston* before her fate was fully revealed, but it does contain the full text of the 1942 Memorial Day message from President Roosevelt to the people of Houston, Texas.

For information about the tactical and strategic contexts in which the light cruiser *Houston* operated, it was logical to turn first to Samuel Eliot Morison, *History of United States Naval Operations in World War II*, vol. 12 (Boston: Little, Brown and Company, 1958), which provides an account of Admiral Halsey's BaitDiv ploy and comprehensive detail about task organization within the U.S. Third Fleet. For symmetry, E. P. Hoyt, in *The Battle of Leyte Gulf: The Death Knell of the Japanese Fleet* (New York: Weybright and Talley, 1972), gives helpful insights into Japanese organizational problems. These are augmented by C. Vann Woodward in *The Battle For Leyte Gulf* (New York: MacMillan, 1947), which contains information from the Japanese side that describes the extraordinary propaganda campaign they launched in October 1944.

Two interesting but little-noted issues are illuminated by secondary sources. Halsey's desire to have as his primary mission the destruction of the Japanese fleet is discussed in E. P. Hoyt, *How They Won the War in the Pacific: Nimitz and His Admirals* (New York: Weybright and Talley, 1970). And the turning point in the demise of Japanese land-based aviation in World War II is documented by W. Karig, R. L. Harris, and F. A. Manson in *Battle Report: The End of an Empire* (New York: Rhinehart and Company, 1948).

Finally, two magazine articles provide sharply drawn battle descriptions from opposite sides of the conflict. Commander W. G. Winslow, in "The Galloping Ghost," U.S. Naval Institute *Proceedings* (Feb 49): 156, recalls early ordeals of the heavy cruiser *Houston* near Java. And Vice Admiral Shigeru Fukudome, in "Strategic Aspects of the Battle Off Formosa," U.S. Naval Institute *Proceedings* (Dec 52): 1292, acknowledges and analyzes Japanese overstatement of battle damage claims in October 1944.